The Famous Tragedy of the Rich Jew of Malta

The Famous Tragedy of the Rich Jew of Malta

Christopher Marlowe

MINT EDITIONS

The Famous Tragedy of the Rich Jew of Malta was first published in 1592.

This edition published by Mint Editions 2021.

ISBN 9781513272061 | E-ISBN 9781513277066

Published by Mint Editions®

MINT EDITIONS

minteditionbooks.com

Publishing Director: Jennifer Newens
Design & Production: Rachel Lopez Metzger
Project Manager: Micaela Clark
Typesetting: Westchester Publishing Services

The Prologue Spoken at Court

Gracious and great, that we so boldly dare
('Mongst other plays that now in fashion are)
To present this, writ many years agone,
And in that age thought second unto none,
We humbly crave your pardon. We pursue
The story of a rich and famous Jew
Who liv'd in Malta: you shall find him still,
In all his projects, a sound Machiavill;
And that's his character. He that hath past
So many censures is now come at last
To have your princely ears: grace you him; then
You crown the action, and renown the pen.

Epilogue Spoken at Court

It is our fear, dread sovereign, we have bin
Too tedious; neither can't be less than sin
To wrong your princely patience: if we have,
Thus low dejected, we your pardon crave;
And, if aught here offend your ear or sight,
We only act and speak what others write.

The Prologue to the Stage, at the Cock-Pit

We know not how our play may pass this stage,
But by the best of poets in that age
The Malta-Jew had being and was made;
And he then by the best of actors play'd:
In Hero and Leander one did gain
A lasting memory; in Tamburlaine,
This Jew, with others many, th' other wan

The attribute of peerless, being a man
Whom we may rank with (doing no one wrong)
Proteus for shapes, and Roscius for a tongue,—
So could he speak, so vary; nor is't hate
To merit in him who doth personate
Our Jew this day; nor is it his ambition
To exceed or equal, being of condition
More modest: this is all that he intends,
(And that too at the urgence of some friends,)
To prove his best, and, if none here gainsay it,
The part he hath studied, and intends to play it.

Epilogue to the Stage, at the Cock-Pit

In graving with Pygmalion to contend,
Or painting with Apelles, doubtless the end
Must be disgrace: our actor did not so,—
He only aim'd to go, but not out-go.
Nor think that this day any prize was play'd;
Here were no bets at all, no wagers laid:
All the ambition that his mind doth swell,
Is but to hear from you (by me) 'twas well.

Dramatis Personae

FERNEZE, governor of Malta.
LODOWICK, his son.
SELIM CALYMATH, son to the Grand Seignior.
MARTIN DEL BOSCO, vice-admiral of Spain.
MATHIAS, a gentleman.
JACOMO, |
BARNARDINE, | friars.
BARABAS, a wealthy Jew.
ITHAMORE, a slave.
PILIA-BORZA, a bully, attendant to BELLAMIRA.

Two Merchants.

Three Jews.

Knights, Bassoes, Officers, Guard, Slaves, Messenger, and Carpenters

KATHARINE, mother to MATHIAS.

ABIGAIL, daughter to BARABAS.

BELLAMIRA, a courtezan.

Abbess.

Nun.

MACHIAVEL as Prologue speaker.

Scene, Malta.

Enter MACHIAVEL.

MACHIAVEL: Albeit the world think Machiavel is dead,
 Yet was his soul but flown beyond the Alps;
 And, now the Guise is dead, is come from France,
 To view this land, and frolic with his friends.
 To some perhaps my name is odious;
 But such as love me, guard me from their tongues,
 And let them know that I am Machiavel,
 And weigh not men, and therefore not men's words.
 Admir'd I am of those that hate me most:
 Though some speak openly against my books,
 Yet will they read me, and thereby attain
 To Peter's chair; and, when they cast me off,
 Are poison'd by my climbing followers.
 I count religion but a childish toy,
 And hold there is no sin but ignorance.
 Birds of the air will tell of murders past!
 I am asham'd to hear such fooleries.
 Many will talk of title to a crown:
 What right had Caesar to the empery?
 Might first made kings, and laws were then most sure
 When, like the Draco's, they were writ in blood.
 Hence comes it that a strong-built citadel
 Commands much more than letters can import:
 Which maxim had Phalaris observ'd,
 H'ad never bellow'd, in a brazen bull,
 Of great ones' envy: o' the poor petty wights
 Let me be envied and not pitied.
 But whither am I bound? I come not, I,
 To read a lecture here in Britain,
 But to present the tragedy of a Jew,
 Who smiles to see how full his bags are cramm'd;
 Which money was not got without my means.
 I crave but this,—grace him as he deserves,
 And let him not be entertain'd the worse
 Because he favours me.
(*Exit*)

Act I

Barabas discovered in his counting-house, with heaps of gold before him.

Barabas: So that of thus much that return was made;
    And of the third part of the Persian ships
    There was the venture summ'd and satisfied.
    As for those Samnites, and the men of Uz,
    That bought my Spanish oils and wines of Greece,
    Here have I purs'd their paltry silverlings.
    Fie, what a trouble 'tis to count this trash!
    Well fare the Arabians, who so richly pay
    The things they traffic for with wedge of gold,
    Whereof a man may easily in a day
    Tell that which may maintain him all his life.
    The needy groom, that never finger'd groat,
    Would make a miracle of thus much coin;
    But he whose steel-barr'd coffers are cramm'd full,
    And all his life-time hath been tired,
    Wearying his fingers' ends with telling it,
    Would in his age be loath to labour so,
    And for a pound to sweat himself to death.
    Give me the merchants of the Indian mines,
    That trade in metal of the purest mould;
    The wealthy Moor, that in the eastern rocks
    Without control can pick his riches up,
    And in his house heap pearl like pebble-stones,
    Receive them free, and sell them by the weight;
    Bags of fiery opals, sapphires, amethysts,
    Jacinths, hard topaz, grass-green emeralds,
    Beauteous rubies, sparkling diamonds,
    And seld-seen costly stones of so great price,
    As one of them, indifferently rated,
    And of a carat of this quantity,
    May serve, in peril of calamity,
    To ransom great kings from captivity.
    This is the ware wherein consists my wealth;

And thus methinks should men of judgment frame
Their means of traffic from the vulgar trade,
And, as their wealth increaseth, so inclose
Infinite riches in a little room.
But now how stands the wind?
Into what corner peers my halcyon's bill?
Ha! to the east? yes. See how stand the vanes—
East and by south: why, then, I hope my ships
I sent for Egypt and the bordering isles
Are gotten up by Nilus' winding banks;
Mine argosy from Alexandria,
Loaden with spice and silks, now under sail,
Are smoothly gliding down by Candy-shore
To Malta, through our Mediterranean sea.—
But who comes here?

Enter a MERCHANT.

How now!

MERCHANT: Barabas, thy ships are safe,
Riding in Malta-road; and all the merchants
With other merchandise are safe arriv'd,
And have sent me to know whether yourself
Will come and custom them.

BARABAS: The ships are safe thou say'st, and richly fraught?

MERCHANT: They are.

BARABAS: Why, then, go bid them come ashore,
And bring with them their bills of entry:
I hope our credit in the custom-house
Will serve as well as I were present there.
Go send 'em threescore camels, thirty mules,
And twenty waggons, to bring up the ware.
But art thou master in a ship of mine,
And is thy credit not enough for that?

MERCHANT: The very custom barely comes to more
Than many merchants of the town are worth,
And therefore far exceeds my credit, sir.

BARABAS: Go tell 'em the Jew of Malta sent thee, man:
Tush, who amongst 'em knows not Barabas?

MERCHANT: I go.

BARABAS: So, then, there's somewhat come.—
    Sirrah, which of my ships art thou master of?
MERCHANT: Of the Speranza, sir.
BARABAS: And saw'st thou not
    Mine argosy at Alexandria?
    Thou couldst not come from Egypt, or by Caire,
    But at the entry there into the sea,
    Where Nilus pays his tribute to the main,
    Thou needs must sail by Alexandria.
MERCHANT: I neither saw them, nor inquir'd of them:
    But this we heard some of our seamen say,
    They wonder'd how you durst with so much wealth
    Trust such a crazed vessel, and so far.
BARABAS: Tush, they are wise! I know her and her strength.
    But go, go thou thy ways, discharge thy ship,
    And bid my factor bring his loading in.
(*Exit* MERCHANT)
    And yet I wonder at this argosy.
Enter a Second MERCHANT.
SECOND MERCHANT: Thine argosy from Alexandria,
    Know, Barabas, doth ride in Malta-road,
    Laden with riches, and exceeding store
    Of Persian silks, of gold, and orient pearl.
BARABAS: How chance you came not with those other ships
    That sail'd by Egypt?
SECOND MERCHANT: Sir, we saw 'em not.
BARABAS: Belike they coasted round by Candy-shore
    About their oils or other businesses.
    But 'twas ill done of you to come so far
    Without the aid or conduct of their ships.
SECOND MERCHANT: Sir, we were wafted by a Spanish fleet,
    That never left us till within a league,
    That had the galleys of the Turk in chase.
BARABAS: O, they were going up to Sicily.
    Well, go,
    And bid the merchants and my men despatch,
    And come ashore, and see the fraught discharg'd.
SECOND MERCHANT: I go.
(*Exit*)

BARABAS: Thus trolls our fortune in by land and sea,
    And thus are we on every side enrich'd:
    These are the blessings promis'd to the Jews,
    And herein was old Abraham's happiness:
    What more may heaven do for earthly man
    Than thus to pour out plenty in their laps,
    Ripping the bowels of the earth for them,
    Making the sea(s) their servants, and the winds
    To drive their substance with successful blasts?
    Who hateth me but for my happiness?
    Or who is honour'd now but for his wealth?
    Rather had I, a Jew, be hated thus,
    Than pitied in a Christian poverty;
    For I can see no fruits in all their faith,
    But malice, falsehood, and excessive pride,
    Which methinks fits not their profession.
    Haply some hapless man hath conscience,
    And for his conscience lives in beggary.
    They say we are a scatter'd nation:
    I cannot tell; but we have scambled up
    More wealth by far than those that brag of faith:
    There's Kirriah Jairim, the great Jew of Greece,
    Obed in Bairseth, Nones in Portugal,
    Myself in Malta, some in Italy,
    Many in France, and wealthy every one;
    Ay, wealthier far than any Christian.
    I must confess we come not to be kings:
    That's not our fault: alas, our number's few!
    And crowns come either by succession,
    Or urg'd by force; and nothing violent,
    Oft have I heard tell, can be permanent.
    Give us a peaceful rule; make Christians kings,
    That thirst so much for principality.
    I have no charge, nor many children,
    But one sole daughter, whom I hold as dear
    As Agamemnon did his Iphigen;
    And all I have is hers.—But who comes here?
Enter three JEWS.
FIRST JEW: Tush, tell not me; 'twas done of policy.

SECOND JEW: Come, therefore, let us go to Barabas;
    For he can counsel best in these affairs:
    And here he comes.
BARABAS: Why, how now, countrymen!
    Why flock you thus to me in multitudes?
    What accident's betided to the Jews?
FIRST JEW: A fleet of warlike galleys, Barabas,
    Are come from Turkey, and lie in our road:
    And they this day sit in the council-house
    To entertain them and their embassy.
BARABAS: Why, let 'em come, so they come not to war;
    Or let 'em war, so we be conquerors.—
    Nay, let 'em combat, conquer, and kill all,
    So they spare me, my daughter, and my wealth.
(*Aside*)
FIRST JEW: Were it for confirmation of a league,
    They would not come in warlike manner thus.
SECOND JEW: I fear their coming will afflict us all.
BARABAS: Fond men, what dream you of their multitudes?
    What need they treat of peace that are in league?
    The Turks and those of Malta are in league:
    Tut, tut, there is some other matter in't.
FIRST JEW: Why, Barabas, they come for peace or war.
BARABAS: Haply for neither, but to pass along,
    Towards Venice, by the Adriatic sea,
    With whom they have attempted many times,
    But never could effect their stratagem.
THIRD JEW: And very wisely said; it may be so.
SECOND JEW: But there's a meeting in the senate-house,
    And all the Jews in Malta must be there.
BARABAS: Hum,—all the Jews in Malta must be there!
    Ay, like enough: why, then, let every man
    Provide him, and be there for fashion-sake.
    If any thing shall there concern our state,
    Assure yourselves I'll look—unto myself.
(*Aside*)
FIRST JEW: I know you will.—Well, brethren, let us go.
SECOND JEW: Let's take our leaves.—Farewell, good Barabas.
BARABAS: Farewell, Zaareth; farewell, Temainte.

      CHRISTOPHER MARLOWE

(*Exeunt* JEWS)

  And, Barabas, now search this secret out;
  Summon thy senses, call thy wits together:
  These silly men mistake the matter clean.
  Long to the Turk did Malta contribute;
  Which tribute all in policy, I fear,
  The Turk has let increase to such a sum
  As all the wealth of Malta cannot pay;
  And now by that advantage thinks, belike,
  To seize upon the town; ay, that he seeks.
  Howe'er the world go, I'll make sure for one,
  And seek in time to intercept the worst,
  Warily guarding that which I ha' got:
  Ego mihimet sum semper proximus:
  Why, let 'em enter, let 'em take the town.

(*Exit*)

Enter FERNEZE *governor of Malta,* KNIGHTS, *and* OFFICERS; *met by*
CALYMATH, *and* BASSOES *of the* TURK.

FERNEZE: Now, bassoes, what demand you at our hands?

FIRST BASSO: Know, knights of Malta, that we came from Rhodes,
  From Cyprus, Candy, and those other isles
  That lie betwixt the Mediterranean seas.

FERNEZE: What's Cyprus, Candy, and those other isles
  To us or Malta? what at our hands demand ye?

CALYMATH: The ten years' tribute that remains unpaid.

FERNEZE: Alas, my lord, the sum is over-great!
  I hope your highness will consider us.

CALYMATH: I wish, grave governor, 'twere in my power
  To favour you; but 'tis my father's cause,
  Wherein I may not, nay, I dare not dally.

FERNEZE: Then give us leave, great Selim Calymath.

CALYMATH: Stand all aside, and let the knights determine;
  And send to keep our galleys under sail,
  For happily we shall not tarry here.—
  Now, governor, how are you resolv'd?

FERNEZE: Thus; since your hard conditions are such
  That you will needs have ten years' tribute past,
  We may have time to make collection
  Amongst the inhabitants of Malta for't.

FIRST BASSO: That's more than is in our commission.

CALYMATH: What, Callapine! a little courtesy:
Let's know their time; perhaps it is not long;
And 'tis more kingly to obtain by peace
Than to enforce conditions by constraint.—
What respite ask you, governor?

FERNEZE: But a month.

CALYMATH: We grant a month; but see you keep your promise.
Now launch our galleys back again to sea,
Where we'll attend the respite you have ta'en,
And for the money send our messenger.
Farewell, great governor, and brave knights of Malta.

FERNEZE: And all good fortune wait on Calymath!

(*Exeunt* CALYMATH *and* BASSOES)

Go one and call those Jews of Malta hither:
Were they not summon'd to appear to-day?

FIRST OFFICER: They were, my lord; and here they come.

Enter BARABAS *and three* JEWS.

FIRST KNIGHT: Have you determin'd what to say to them?

FERNEZE: Yes; give me leave:—and, Hebrews, now come near.
From the Emperor of Turkey is arriv'd
Great Selim Calymath, his highness' son,
To levy of us ten years' tribute past:
Now, then, here know that it concerneth us.

BARABAS: Then, good my lord, to keep your quiet still,
Your lordship shall do well to let them have it.

FERNEZE: Soft, Barabas! there's more 'longs to't than so.
To what this ten years' tribute will amount,
That we have cast, but cannot compass it
By reason of the wars, that robb'd our store;
And therefore are we to request your aid.

BARABAS: Alas, my lord, we are no soldiers!
And what's our aid against so great a prince?

FIRST KNIGHT: Tut, Jew, we know thou art no soldier:
Thou art a merchant and a money'd man,
And 'tis thy money, Barabas, we seek.

BARABAS: How, my lord! my money!

FERNEZE: Thine and the rest;
For, to be short, amongst you't must be had.

CHRISTOPHER MARLOWE

First Jew: Alas, my lord, the most of us are poor!

Ferneze: Then let the rich increase your portions.

Barabas: Are strangers with your tribute to be tax'd?

Second Knight: Have strangers leave with us to get their wealth?
Then let them with us contribute.

Barabas: How! equally?

Ferneze: No, Jew, like infidels;
For through our sufferance of your hateful lives,
Who stand accursed in the sight of heaven,
These taxes and afflictions are befall'n,
And therefore thus we are determined.—
Read there the articles of our decrees.

Officer: (*reads*) First, The Tribute-Money Of The Turks
Shall All Be Levied Amongst The Jews, And Each Of
Them To Pay One Half Of His Estate.

Barabas: How! half his estate!—I hope you mean not mine.
(*Aside*)

Ferneze: Read on.

Officer: (*reads*) Secondly, He That Denies To Pay, Shall
Straight-Become A Christian.

Barabas: How! a Christian!—Hum,—what's here to do?
(*Aside*)

Officer: (*reads*) Lastly, He That Denies This, Shall
Absolutely Lose All He Has.

Three Jews: O my lord, we will give half!

Barabas: O earth-mettled villains, and no Hebrews born!
And will you basely thus submit yourselves
To leave your goods to their arbitrement?

Ferneze: Why, Barabas, wilt thou be christened?

Barabas: No, governor, I will be no convertite.

Ferneze: Then pay thy half.

Barabas: Why, know you what you did by this device?
Half of my substance is a city's wealth.
Governor, it was not got so easily;
Nor will I part so slightly therewithal.

Ferneze: Sir, half is the penalty of our decree;
Either pay that, or we will seize on all.

Barabas: Corpo di Dio! stay: you shall have half;
Let me be us'd but as my brethren are.

FERNEZE: No, Jew, thou hast denied the articles,
    And now it cannot be recall'd.
(*Exeunt* OFFICERS, *on a sign from* FERNEZE)
BARABAS: Will you, then, steal my goods?
    Is theft the ground of your religion?
FERNEZE: No, Jew; we take particularly thine,
    To save the ruin of a multitude:
    And better one want for a common good,
    Than many perish for a private man:
    Yet, Barabas, we will not banish thee,
    But here in Malta, where thou gott'st thy wealth,
    Live still; and, if thou canst, get more.
BARABAS: Christians, what or how can I multiply?
    Of naught is nothing made.
FIRST KNIGHT: From naught at first thou cam'st to little
    wealth,
    From little unto more, from more to most:
    If your first curse fall heavy on thy head,
    And make thee poor and scorn'd of all the world,
    'Tis not our fault, but thy inherent sin.
BARABAS: What, bring you Scripture to confirm your
    wrongs?
    Preach me not out of my possessions.
    Some Jews are wicked, as all Christians are:
    But say the tribe that I descended of
    Were all in general cast away for sin,
    Shall I be tried by their transgression?
    The man that dealeth righteously shall live;
    And which of you can charge me otherwise?
FERNEZE: Out, wretched Barabas!
    Sham'st thou not thus to justify thyself,
    As if we knew not thy profession?
    If thou rely upon thy righteousness,
    Be patient, and thy riches will increase.
    Excess of wealth is cause of covetousness;
    And covetousness, O, 'tis a monstrous sin!
BARABAS: Ay, but theft is worse: tush! take not from me, then,
    For that is theft; and, if you rob me thus,
    I must be forc'd to steal, and compass more.

CHRISTOPHER MARLOWE

FIRST KNIGHT: Grave governor, list not to his exclaims:
    Convert his mansion to a nunnery;
    His house will harbour many holy nuns.
FERNEZE: It shall be so.
Re-enter OFFICERS.
    Now, officers, have you done?
FIRST OFFICER: Ay, my lord, we have seiz'd upon the goods
    And wares of Barabas, which, being valu'd,
    Amount to more than all the wealth in Malta:
    And of the other we have seized half.
FERNEZE: Then we'll take order for the residue.
BARABAS: Well, then, my lord, say, are you satisfied?
    You have my goods, my money, and my wealth,
    My ships, my store, and all that I enjoy'd;
    And, having all, you can request no more,
    Unless your unrelenting flinty hearts
    Suppress all pity in your stony breasts,
    And now shall move you to bereave my life.
FERNEZE: No, Barabas; to stain our hands with blood
    Is far from us and our profession.
BARABAS: Why, I esteem the injury far less,
    To take the lives of miserable men
    Than be the causers of their misery.
    You have my wealth, the labour of my life,
    The comfort of mine age, my children's hope;
    And therefore ne'er distinguish of the wrong.
FERNEZE: Content thee, Barabas; thou hast naught but right.
BARABAS: Your extreme right does me exceeding wrong:
    But take it to you, i'the devil's name!
FERNEZE: Come, let us in, and gather of these goods
    The money for this tribute of the Turk.
FIRST KNIGHT: 'Tis necessary that be look'd unto;
    For, if we break our day, we break the league,
    And that will prove but simple policy.
(*Exeunt all except* BARABAS *and the three* JEWS)
BARABAS: Ay, policy! that's their profession,
    And not simplicity, as they suggest.—
    The plagues of Egypt, and the curse of heaven,
    Earth's barrenness, and all men's hatred,

Inflict upon them, thou great Primus Motor!
And here upon my knees, striking the earth,
I ban their souls to everlasting pains,
And extreme tortures of the fiery deep,
That thus have dealt with me in my distress!

FIRST JEW: O, yet be patient, gentle Barabas!

BARABAS: O silly brethren, born to see this day,
Why stand you thus unmov'd with my laments?
Why weep you not to think upon my wrongs?
Why pine not I, and die in this distress?

FIRST JEW: Why, Barabas, as hardly can we brook
The cruel handling of ourselves in this:
Thou seest they have taken half our goods.

BARABAS: Why did you yield to their extortion?
You were a multitude, and I but one;
And of me only have they taken all.

FIRST JEW: Yet, brother Barabas, remember Job.

BARABAS: What tell you me of Job? I wot his wealth
Was written thus; he had seven thousand sheep,
Three thousand camels, and two hundred yoke
Of labouring oxen, and five hundred
She-asses: but for every one of those,
Had they been valu'd at indifferent rate,
I had at home, and in mine argosy,
And other ships that came from Egypt last,
As much as would have bought his beasts and him,
And yet have kept enough to live upon;
So that not he, but I, may curse the day,
Thy fatal birth-day, forlorn Barabas;
And henceforth wish for an eternal night,
That clouds of darkness may inclose my flesh,
And hide these extreme sorrows from mine eyes;
For only I have toil'd to inherit here
The months of vanity, and loss of time,
And painful nights, have been appointed me.

SECOND JEW: Good Barabas, be patient.

BARABAS: Ay, I pray, leave me in my patience. You, that
Were ne'er possess'd of wealth, are pleas'd with want;
But give him liberty at least to mourn,

That in a field, amidst his enemies,
Doth see his soldiers slain, himself disarm'd,
And knows no means of his recovery:
Ay, let me sorrow for this sudden chance;
'Tis in the trouble of my spirit I speak:
Great injuries are not so soon forgot.

FIRST JEW: Come, let us leave him; in his ireful mood
Our words will but increase his ecstasy.

SECOND JEW: On, then: but, trust me, 'tis a misery
To see a man in such affliction.—
Farewell, Barabas.

BARABAS: Ay, fare you well.

(*Exeunt three* JEWS)

See the simplicity of these base slaves,
Who, for the villains have no wit themselves,
Think me to be a senseless lump of clay,
That will with every water wash to dirt!
No, Barabas is born to better chance,
And fram'd of finer mould than common men,
That measure naught but by the present time.
A reaching thought will search his deepest wits,
And cast with cunning for the time to come;
For evils are apt to happen every day.

Enter ABIGAIL.

But whither wends my beauteous Abigail?
O, what has made my lovely daughter sad?
What, woman! moan not for a little loss;
Thy father has enough in store for thee.

ABIGAIL: Nor for myself, but aged Barabas,
Father, for thee lamenteth Abigail:
But I will learn to leave these fruitless tears;
And, urg'd thereto with my afflictions,
With fierce exclaims run to the senate-house,
And in the senate reprehend them all,
And rent their hearts with tearing of my hair,
Till they reduce the wrongs done to my father.

BARABAS: No, Abigail; things past recovery
Are hardly cur'd with exclamations:
Be silent, daughter; sufferance breeds ease,

And time may yield us an occasion,
Which on the sudden cannot serve the turn.
Besides, my girl, think me not all so fond
As negligently to forgo so much
Without provision for thyself and me:
Ten thousand portagues, besides great pearls,
Rich costly jewels, and stones infinite,
Fearing the worst of this before it fell,
I closely hid.

ABIGAIL: Where, father?

BARABAS: In my house, my girl.

ABIGAIL: Then shall they ne'er be seen of Barabas;
For they have seiz'd upon thy house and wares.

BARABAS: But they will give me leave once more, I trow,
To go into my house.

ABIGAIL: That may they not;
For there I left the governor placing nuns,
Displacing me; and of thy house they mean
To make a nunnery, where none but their own sect
Must enter in; men generally barr'd.

BARABAS: My gold, my gold, and all my wealth is gone!—
You partial heavens, have I deserv'd this plague?
What, will you thus oppose me, luckless stars,
To make me desperate in my poverty?
And, knowing me impatient in distress,
Think me so mad as I will hang myself,
That I may vanish o'er the earth in air,
And leave no memory that e'er I was?
No, I will live; nor loathe I this my life:
And, since you leave me in the ocean thus
To sink or swim, and put me to my shifts,
I'll rouse my senses, and awake myself.—
Daughter, I have it: thou perceiv'st the plight
Wherein these Christians have oppressed me:
Be rul'd by me, for in extremity
We ought to make bar of no policy.

ABIGAIL: Father, whate'er it be, to injure them
That have so manifestly wronged us,

What will not Abigail attempt?

BARABAS: Why, so.
    Then thus: thou told'st me they have turn'd my house
    Into a nunnery, and some nuns are there?

ABIGAIL: I did.

BARABAS: Then, Abigail, there must my girl
    Entreat the abbess to be entertain'd.

ABIGAIL: How! as a nun?

BARABAS: Ay, daughter; for religion
    Hides many mischiefs from suspicion.

ABIGAIL: Ay, but, father, they will suspect me there.

BARABAS: Let 'em suspect; but be thou so precise
    As they may think it done of holiness:
    Entreat 'em fair, and give them friendly speech,
    And seem to them as if thy sins were great,
    Till thou hast gotten to be entertain'd.

ABIGAIL: Thus, father, shall I much dissemble.

BARABAS: Tush!
    As good dissemble that thou never mean'st,
    As first mean truth and then dissemble it:
    A counterfeit profession is better
    Than unseen hypocrisy.

ABIGAIL: Well, father, say I be entertain'd,
    What then shall follow?

BARABAS: This shall follow then.
    There have I hid, close underneath the plank
    That runs along the upper-chamber floor,
    The gold and jewels which I kept for thee:—
    But here they come: be cunning, Abigail.

ABIGAIL: Then, father, go with me.

BARABAS: No, Abigail, in this
    It is not necessary I be seen;
    For I will seem offended with thee for't:
    Be close, my girl, for this must fetch my gold.

(*They retire*)

Enter FRIAR JACOMO, FRIAR BARNARDINE, ABBESS, *and a* NUN.

FRIAR JACOMO: Sisters,
    We now are almost at the new-made nunnery.

ABBESS: The better; for we love not to be seen:
  'Tis thirty winters long since some of us
  Did stray so far amongst the multitude.
FRIAR JACOMO: But, madam, this house
  And waters of this new-made nunnery
  Will much delight you.
ABBESS: It may be so.—But who comes here?
(ABIGAIL *comes forward*)
ABIGAIL: Grave abbess, and you happy virgins' guide,
  Pity the state of a distressed maid!
ABBESS: What art thou, daughter?
ABIGAIL: The hopeless daughter of a hapless Jew,
  The Jew of Malta, wretched Barabas,
  Sometimes the owner of a goodly house,
  Which they have now turn'd to a nunnery.
ABBESS: Well, daughter, say, what is thy suit with us?
ABIGAIL: Fearing the afflictions which my father feels
  Proceed from sin or want of faith in us,
  I'd pass away my life in penitence,
  And be a novice in your nunnery,
  To make atonement for my labouring soul.
FRIAR JACOMO: No doubt, brother, but this proceedeth of the spirit.
FRIAR BARNARDINE: Ay, and of a moving spirit too, brother: but come,
  Let us entreat she may be entertain'd.
ABBESS: Well, daughter, we admit you for a nun.
ABIGAIL: First let me as a novice learn to frame
  My solitary life to your strait laws,
  And let me lodge where I was wont to lie:
  I do not doubt, by your divine precepts
  And mine own industry, but to profit much.
BARABAS: As much, I hope, as all I hid is worth.
(*Aside*)
ABBESS: Come, daughter, follow us.
BARABAS: (*coming forward*) Why, how now, Abigail!
  What mak'st thou 'mongst these hateful Christians?
FRIAR JACOMO: Hinder her not, thou man of little faith,
  For she has mortified herself.
BARABAS: How! mortified!
FRIAR JACOMO: And is admitted to the sisterhood.

CHRISTOPHER MARLOWE

BARABAS: Child of perdition, and thy father's shame!
    What wilt thou do among these hateful fiends?
    I charge thee on my blessing that thou leave
    These devils and their damned heresy!
ABIGAIL: Father, forgive me—
BARABAS: Nay, back, Abigail,
    And think upon the jewels and the gold;
    The board is marked thus that covers it.—
(*Aside to* ABIGAIL *in a whisper*)
    Away, accursed, from thy father's sight!
FRIAR JACOMO: Barabas, although thou art in misbelief,
    And wilt not see thine own afflictions,
    Yet let thy daughter be no longer blind.
BARABAS: Blind friar, I reck not thy persuasions,—
    The board is marked thus that covers it—
(*Aside to* ABIGAIL *in a whisper*)
    For I had rather die than see her thus.—
    Wilt thou forsake me too in my distress,
    Seduced daughter?—Go, forget not.—
(*Aside to her in a whisper*)
    Becomes it Jews to be so credulous?—
    To-morrow early I'll be at the door.—
(*Aside to her in a whisper*)
    No, come not at me; if thou wilt be damn'd,
    Forget me, see me not; and so, be gone!—
    Farewell; remember to-morrow morning.—
(*Aside to her in a whisper*)
    Out, out, thou wretch!
(*Exit, on one side,* BARABAS. *Exeunt, on the other side,* FRIARS, ABBESS,
NUN, *and* ABIGAIL: *and, as they are going out,*)
Enter MATHIAS.
MATHIAS: Who's this? fair Abigail, the rich Jew's daughter,
    Become a nun! her father's sudden fall
    Has humbled her, and brought her down to this:
    Tut, she were fitter for a tale of love,
    Than to be tired out with orisons;
    And better would she far become a bed,
    Embraced in a friendly lover's arms,
    Than rise at midnight to a solemn mass.

Enter LODOWICK.

LODOWICK: Why, how now, Don Mathias! in a dump?

MATHIAS: Believe me, noble Lodowick, I have seen
    The strangest sight, in my opinion,
    That ever I beheld.

LODOWICK: What was't, I prithee?

MATHIAS: A fair young maid, scarce fourteen years of age,
    The sweetest flower in Cytherea's field,
    Cropt from the pleasures of the fruitful earth,
    And strangely metamorphos'd (*to a*) nun.

LODOWICK: But say, what was she?

MATHIAS: Why, the rich Jew's daughter.

LODOWICK: What, Barabas, whose goods were lately seiz'd?
    Is she so fair?

MATHIAS: And matchless beautiful,
    As, had you seen her, 'twould have mov'd your heart,
    Though countermin'd with walls of brass, to love,
    Or, at the least, to pity.

LODOWICK: An if she be so fair as you report,
    'Twere time well spent to go and visit her:
    How say you? shall we?

MATHIAS: I must and will, sir; there's no remedy.

LODOWICK: And so will I too, or it shall go hard.
    Farewell, Mathias.

MATHIAS: Farewell, Lodowick.

(*Exeunt severally*)

Act II

Enter BARABAS, *with a light.*

BARABAS: Thus, like the sad-presaging raven, that
    tolls
    The sick man's passport in her hollow beak,
    And in the shadow of the silent night
    Doth shake contagion from her sable wings,
    Vex'd and tormented runs poor Barabas
    With fatal curses towards these Christians.
    The incertain pleasures of swift-footed time
    Have ta'en their flight, and left me in despair;
    And of my former riches rests no more
    But bare remembrance; like a soldier's scar,
    That has no further comfort for his maim.—
    O Thou, that with a fiery pillar ledd'st
    The sons of Israel through the dismal shades,
    Light Abraham's offspring; and direct the hand
    Of Abigail this night! or let the day
    Turn to eternal darkness after this!—
    No sleep can fasten on my watchful eyes,
    Nor quiet enter my distemper'd thoughts,
    Till I have answer of my Abigail.
Enter ABIGAIL *above.*
ABIGAIL: Now have I happily espied a time
    To search the plank my father did appoint;
    And here, behold, unseen, where I have found
    The gold, the pearls, and jewels, which he hid.
BARABAS: Now I remember those old women's words,
    Who in my wealth would tell me winter's tales,
    And speak of spirits and ghosts that glide by night
    About the place where treasure hath been hid:
    And now methinks that I am one of those;
    For, whilst I live, here lives my soul's sole hope,
    And, when I die, here shall my spirit walk.
ABIGAIL: Now that my father's fortune were so good
    As but to be about this happy place!

'Tis not so happy: yet, when we parted last,
He said he would attend me in the morn.
Then, gentle Sleep, where'er his body rests,
Give charge to Morpheus that he may dream
A golden dream, and of the sudden wake,
Come and receive the treasure I have found.

BARABAS: Bueno para todos mi ganado no era:
As good go on, as sit so sadly thus.—
But stay: what star shines yonder in the east?
The loadstar of my life, if Abigail.—
Who's there?

ABIGAIL: Who's that?

BARABAS: Peace, Abigail! 'tis I.

ABIGAIL: Then, father, here receive thy happiness.

BARABAS: Hast thou't?

ABIGAIL: Here. (*throws down bags*) Hast thou't?
There's more, and more, and more.

BARABAS: O my girl,
My gold, my fortune, my felicity,
Strength to my soul, death to mine enemy;
Welcome the first beginner of my bliss!
O Abigail, Abigail, that I had thee here too!
Then my desires were fully satisfied:
But I will practice thy enlargement thence:
O girl! O gold! O beauty! O my bliss!

(*Hugs the bags*)

ABIGAIL: Father, it draweth towards midnight now,
And 'bout this time the nuns begin to wake;
To shun suspicion, therefore, let us part.

BARABAS: Farewell, my joy, and by my fingers take
A kiss from him that sends it from his soul.

(*Exit* ABIGAIL *above*)

Now, Phoebus, ope the eye-lids of the day.
And, for the raven, wake the morning lark,
That I may hover with her in the air,
Singing o'er these, as she does o'er her young.
Hermoso placer de los dineros.

(*Exit*)

Enter FERNEZE, MARTIN DEL BOSCO, KNIGHTS, *and* OFFICERS.

CHRISTOPHER MARLOWE

FERNEZE: Now, captain, tell us whither thou art bound?
  Whence is thy ship that anchors in our road?
  And why thou cam'st ashore without our leave?
MARTIN DEL BOSCO: Governor of Malta, hither am I bound;
  My ship, the Flying Dragon, is of Spain,
  And so am I; Del Bosco is my name,
  Vice-admiral unto the Catholic King.
FIRST KNIGHT: 'Tis true, my lord; therefore entreat him well.
MARTIN DEL BOSCO: Our fraught is Grecians, Turks, and Afric
  Moors;
  For late upon the coast of Corsica,
  Because we vail'd not to the Turkish fleet,
  Their creeping galleys had us in the chase:
  But suddenly the wind began to rise,
  And then we luff'd and tack'd, and fought at ease:
  Some have we fir'd, and many have we sunk;
  But one amongst the rest became our prize:
  The captain's slain; the rest remain our slaves,
  Of whom we would make sale in Malta here.
FERNEZE: Martin del Bosco, I have heard of thee:
  Welcome to Malta, and to all of us!
  But to admit a sale of these thy Turks,
  We may not, nay, we dare not give consent,
  By reason of a tributary league.
FIRST KNIGHT: Del Bosco, as thou lov'st and honour'st us,
  Persuade our governor against the Turk:
  This truce we have is but in hope of gold,
  And with that sum he craves might we wage war.
MARTIN DEL BOSCO: Will knights of Malta be in league with Turks,
  And buy it basely too for sums of gold?
  My lord, remember that, to Europe's shame,
  The Christian isle of Rhodes, from whence you came,
  Was lately lost, and you were stated here
  To be at deadly enmity with Turks.
FERNEZE: Captain, we know it; but our force is small.
MARTIN DEL BOSCO: What is the sum that Calymath requires?
FERNEZE: A hundred thousand crowns.
MARTIN DEL BOSCO: My lord and king hath title to this isle,
  And he means quickly to expel you hence;

Therefore be rul'd by me, and keep the gold:
I'll write unto his majesty for aid,
And not depart until I see you free.

FERNEZE: On this condition shall thy Turks be sold.—
Go, officers, and set them straight in show.—

(*Exeunt* OFFICERS)

Bosco, thou shalt be Malta's general;
We and our warlike knights will follow thee
Against these barbarous misbelieving Turks.

MARTIN DEL BOSCO: So shall you imitate those you succeed;
For, when their hideous force environ'd Rhodes,
Small though the number was that kept the town,
They fought it out, and not a man surviv'd
To bring the hapless news to Christendom.

FERNEZE: So will we fight it out: come, let's away.
Proud daring Calymath, instead of gold,
We'll send thee bullets wrapt in smoke and fire:
Claim tribute where thou wilt, we are resolv'd,—
Honour is bought with blood, and not with gold.

(*Exeunt*)

Enter OFFICERS, *with* ITHAMORE *and other* SLAVES.

FIRST OFFICER: This is the market-place; here let 'em stand:
Fear not their sale, for they'll be quickly bought.

SECOND OFFICER: Every one's price is written on his back,
And so much must they yield, or not be sold.

FIRST OFFICER:
Here comes the Jew: had not his goods been seiz'd,
He'd give us present money for them all.

Enter BARABAS.

BARABAS: In spite of these swine-eating Christians,
(*Unchosen nation, never circumcis'd,*
Poor villains, such as were ne'er thought upon
Till Titus and Vespasian conquer'd us)
Am I become as wealthy as I was.
They hop'd my daughter would ha' been a nun;
But she's at home, and I have bought a house
As great and fair as is the governor's:
And there, in spite of Malta, will I dwell,
Having Ferneze's hand; whose heart I'll have,

Ay, and his son's too, or it shall go hard.
I am not of the tribe of Levi, I,
That can so soon forget an injury.
We Jews can fawn like spaniels when we please;
And when we grin we bite; yet are our looks
As innocent and harmless as a lamb's.
I learn'd in Florence how to kiss my hand,
Heave up my shoulders when they call me dog,
And duck as low as any bare-foot friar;
Hoping to see them starve upon a stall,
Or else be gather'd for in our synagogue,
That, when the offering-basin comes to me,
Even for charity I may spit into't.—
Here comes Don Lodowick, the governor's son,
One that I love for his good father's sake.

Enter LODOWICK.

LODOWICK: I hear the wealthy Jew walked this way:
    I'll seek him out, and so insinuate,
    That I may have a sight of Abigail,
    For Don Mathias tells me she is fair.

BARABAS: Now will I shew myself to have more of the serpent than
    the dove; that is, more knave than fool.

(*Aside*)

LODOWICK: Yond' walks the Jew: now for fair Abigail.

BARABAS: Ay, ay, no doubt but she's at your command.

(*Aside*)

LODOWICK: Barabas, thou know'st I am the governor's son.

BARABAS: I would you were his father too, sir! that's all the harm
    I wish you.—The slave looks like a hog's cheek new-singed.

(*Aside*)

LODOWICK: Whither walk'st thou, Barabas?

BARABAS: No further: 'tis a custom held with us,
    That when we speak with Gentiles like to you,
    We turn into the air to purge ourselves;
    For unto us the promise doth belong.

LODOWICK: Well, Barabas, canst help me to a diamond?

BARABAS: O, sir, your father had my diamonds:
    Yet I have one left that will serve your turn.—
    I mean my daughter; but, ere he shall have her,

I'll sacrifice her on a pile of wood:
I ha' the poison of the city for him,
And the white leprosy.
(*Aside*)
LODOWICK: What sparkle does it give without a foil?
BARABAS: The diamond that I talk of ne'er was foil'd:—
But, when he touches it, it will be foil'd.—
(*Aside*)
Lord Lodowick, it sparkles bright and fair.
LODOWICK: Is it square or pointed? pray, let me know.
BARABAS: Pointed it is, good sir,—but not for you.
(*Aside*)
LODOWICK: I like it much the better.
BARABAS: So do I too.
LODOWICK: How shews it by night?
BARABAS: Outshines Cynthia's rays:—
You'll like it better far o' nights than days.
(*Aside*)
LODOWICK: And what's the price?
BARABAS: Your life, an if you have it (*Aside*)—O my lord,
We will not jar about the price: come to my house,
And I will give't your honour—with a vengeance.
(*Aside*)
LODOWICK: No, Barabas, I will deserve it first.
BARABAS: Good sir,
Your father has deserv'd it at my hands,
Who, of mere charity and Christian ruth,
To bring me to religious purity,
And, as it were, in catechising sort,
To make me mindful of my mortal sins,
Against my will, and whether I would or no,
Seiz'd all I had, and thrust me out o' doors,
And made my house a place for nuns most chaste.
LODOWICK: No doubt your soul shall reap the fruit of it.
BARABAS: Ay, but, my lord, the harvest is far off:
And yet I know the prayers of those nuns
And holy friars, having money for their pains,
Are wondrous;—and indeed do no man good;—
(*Aside*)

And, seeing they are not idle, but still doing,
'Tis likely they in time may reap some fruit,
I mean, in fullness of perfection.

LODOWICK: Good Barabas, glance not at our holy nuns.

BARABAS: No, but I do it through a burning zeal,—
Hoping ere long to set the house a-fire;
For, though they do a while increase and multiply,
I'll have a saying to that nunnery.—

(*Aside*)

As for the diamond, sir, I told you of,
Come home, and there's no price shall make us part,
Even for your honourable father's sake,—
It shall go hard but I will see your death.—

(*Aside*)

But now I must be gone to buy a slave.

LODOWICK: And, Barabas, I'll bear thee company.

BARABAS: Come, then; here's the market-place.—
What's the price of this slave? two hundred crowns! do the Turks
weigh so much?

FIRST OFFICER: Sir, that's his price.

BARABAS: What, can he steal, that you demand so much?
Belike he has some new trick for a purse;
An if he has, he is worth three hundred plates,
So that, being bought, the town-seal might be got
To keep him for his life-time from the gallows:
The sessions-day is critical to thieves,
And few or none scape but by being purg'd.

LODOWICK: Rat'st thou this Moor but at two hundred plates?

FIRST OFFICER: No more, my lord.

BARABAS: Why should this Turk be dearer than that Moor?

FIRST OFFICER: Because he is young, and has more qualities.

BARABAS: What, hast the philosopher's stone? an thou hast, break my
head with it, I'll forgive thee.

SLAVE: No, sir; I can cut and shave.

BARABAS: Let me see, sirrah; are you not an old shaver?

SLAVE: Alas, sir, I am a very youth!

BARABAS: A youth! I'll buy you, and marry you to Lady Vanity, if you
do well.

SLAVE: I will serve you, sir.

BARABAS: Some wicked trick or other: it may be, under colour of
shaving, thou'lt cut my throat for my goods. Tell me, hast thou thy
health well?

SLAVE: Ay, passing well.

BARABAS: So much the worse: I must have one that's sickly, an't be but
for sparing victuals: 'tis not a stone of beef a-day will maintain you
in these chops.—Let me see one that's somewhat leaner.

FIRST OFFICER: Here's a leaner; how like you him?

BARABAS: Where wast thou born?

ITHAMORE: In Thrace; brought up in Arabia.

BARABAS: So much the better; thou art for my turn.

An hundred crowns? I'll have him; there's the coin.

(*Gives money*)

FIRST OFFICER: Then mark him, sir, and take him hence.

BARABAS: Ay, mark him, you were best; for this is he
That by my help shall do much villany.—

(*Aside*)

My lord, farewell.—Come, sirrah; you are mine.—
As for the diamond, it shall be yours:
I pray, sir, be no stranger at my house;
All that I have shall be at your command.

Enter MATHIAS *and* KATHARINE.

MATHIAS: What make the Jew and Lodowick so private?
I fear me 'tis about fair Abigail.

(*Aside*)

BARABAS: (*to* LODOWICK) Yonder comes Don Mathias; let us stay:
He loves my daughter, and she holds him dear;
But I have sworn to frustrate both their hopes,
And be reveng'd upon the—governor.

(*Aside*)

(*Exit* LODOWICK)

KATHARINE: This Moor is comeliest, is he not? speak, son.

MATHIAS: No, this is the better, mother, view this well.

BARABAS: Seem not to know me here before your mother,
Lest she mistrust the match that is in hand:
When you have brought her home, come to my house;
Think of me as thy father: son, farewell.

MATHIAS: But wherefore talk'd Don Lodowick with you?

BARABAS: Tush, man! we talk'd of diamonds, not of Abigail.

CHRISTOPHER MARLOWE

KATHARINE: Tell me, Mathias, is not that the Jew?

BARABAS: As for the comment on the Maccabees,
  I have it, sir, and 'tis at your command.

MATHIAS: Yes, madam, and my talk with him was
  About the borrowing of a book or two.

KATHARINE: Converse not with him; he is cast off from heaven.—
  Thou hast thy crowns, fellow.—Come, let's away.

MATHIAS: Sirrah Jew, remember the book.

BARABAS: Marry, will I, sir.

(*Exeunt* KATHARLNE *and* MATHIAS)

FIRST OFFICER: Come, I have made a reasonable market; let's away.

(*Exeunt* OFFICERS *with* SLAVES)

BARABAS: Now let me know thy name, and therewithal
  Thy birth, condition, and profession.

ITHAMORE: Faith, sir, my birth is but mean; my name's Ithamore; my
  profession what you please.

BARABAS: Hast thou no trade? then listen to my words,
  And I will teach (*thee*) that shall stick by thee:
  First, be thou void of these affections,
  Compassion, love, vain hope, and heartless fear;
  Be mov'd at nothing, see thou pity none,
  But to thyself smile when the Christians moan.

ITHAMORE: O, brave, master! I worship your nose for this.

BARABAS: As for myself, I walk abroad o' nights,
  And kill sick people groaning under walls:
  Sometimes I go about and poison wells;
  And now and then, to cherish Christian thieves,
  I am content to lose some of my crowns,
  That I may, walking in my gallery,
  See 'em go pinion'd along by my door.
  Being young, I studied physic, and began
  To practice first upon the Italian;
  There I enrich'd the priests with burials,
  And always kept the sexton's arms in ure
  With digging graves and ringing dead men's knells:
  And, after that, was I an engineer,
  And in the wars 'twixt France and Germany,
  Under pretence of helping Charles the Fifth,
  Slew friend and enemy with my stratagems:

Then, after that, was I an usurer,
And with extorting, cozening, forfeiting,
And tricks belonging unto brokery,
I fill'd the gaols with bankrupts in a year,
And with young orphans planted hospitals;
And every moon made some or other mad,
And now and then one hang himself for grief,
Pinning upon his breast a long great scroll
How I with interest tormented him.
But mark how I am blest for plaguing them;—
I have as much coin as will buy the town.
But tell me now, how hast thou spent thy time?

ITHAMORE: Faith, master,
In setting Christian villages on fire,
Chaining of eunuchs, binding galley-slaves.
One time I was an hostler in an inn,
And in the night-time secretly would I steal
To travellers' chambers, and there cut their throats:
Once at Jerusalem, where the pilgrims kneel'd,
I strewed powder on the marble stones,
And therewithal their knees would rankle so,
That I have laugh'd a-good to see the cripples
Go limping home to Christendom on stilts.

BARABAS: Why, this is something: make account of me
As of thy fellow; we are villains both;
Both circumcised; we hate Christians both:
Be true and secret; thou shalt want no gold.
But stand aside; here comes Don Lodowick.

Enter LODOWICK.

LODOWICK: O, Barabas, well met;
Where is the diamond you told me of?

BARABAS: I have it for you, sir: please you walk in with me.—
What, ho, Abigail! open the door, I say!

Enter ABIGAIL, *with letters.*

ABIGAIL: In good time, father; here are letters come
From Ormus, and the post stays here within.

BARABAS: Give me the letters.—Daughter, do you hear?
Entertain Lodowick, the governor's son,
With all the courtesy you can afford,

Provided that you keep your maidenhead:
Use him as if he were a Philistine;
Dissemble, swear, protest, vow love to him:
He is not of the seed of Abraham.—
(*Aside to her*)
I am a little busy, sir; pray, pardon me.—
Abigail, bid him welcome for my sake.
ABIGAIL: For your sake and his own he's welcome hither.
BARABAS: Daughter, a word more: kiss him, speak him fair,
  And like a cunning Jew so cast about,
  That ye be both made sure ere you come out.
(*Aside to her*)
ABIGAIL: O father, Don Mathias is my love!
BARABAS: I know it: yet, I say, make love to him;
  Do, it is requisite it should be so.—
(*Aside to her*)
  Nay, on my life, it is my factor's hand;
  But go you in, I'll think upon the account.
(*Exeunt* ABIGAIL *and* LODOWICK *into the house*)
  The account is made, for Lodovico dies.
  My factor sends me word a merchant's fled
  That owes me for a hundred tun of wine:
  I weigh it thus much (*snapping his fingers*)! I have wealth enough;
  For now by this has he kiss'd Abigail,
  And she vows love to him, and he to her.
  As sure as heaven rain'd manna for the Jews,
  So sure shall he and Don Mathias die:
  His father was my chiefest enemy.
Enter MATHIAS.
  Whither goes Don Mathias? stay a while.
MATHIAS: Whither, but to my fair love Abigail?
BARABAS: Thou know'st, and heaven can witness it is true,
  That I intend my daughter shall be thine.
MATHIAS: Ay, Barabas, or else thou wrong'st me much.
BARABAS: O, heaven forbid I should have such a thought!
  Pardon me though I weep: the governor's son
  Will, whether I will or no, have Abigail;
  He sends her letters, bracelets, jewels, rings.
MATHIAS: Does she receive them?

BARABAS: She! no, Mathias, no, but sends them back;
    And, when he comes, she locks herself up fast;
    Yet through the key-hole will he talk to her,
    While she runs to the window, looking out
    When you should come and hale him from the door.
MATHIAS: O treacherous Lodowick!
BARABAS: Even now, as I came home, he slipt me in,
    And I am sure he is with Abigail.
MATHIAS: I'll rouse him thence.
BARABAS: Not for all Malta; therefore sheathe your sword;
    If you love me, no quarrels in my house;
    But steal you in, and seem to see him not:
    I'll give him such a warning ere he goes,
    As he shall have small hopes of Abigail.
    Away, for here they come.
Re-enter LODOWICK *and* ABIGAIL.
MATHIAS: What, hand in hand! I cannot suffer this.
BARABAS: Mathias, as thou lov'st me, not a word.
MATHIAS: Well, let it pass; another time shall serve.
(*Exit into the house*)
LODOWICK: Barabas, is not that the widow's son?
BARABAS: Ay, and take heed, for he hath sworn your death.
LODOWICK: My death! what, is the base-born peasant mad?
BARABAS: No, no; but happily he stands in fear
    Of that which you, I think, ne'er dream upon,—
    My daughter here, a paltry silly girl.
LODOWICK: Why, loves she Don Mathias?
BARABAS: Doth she not with her smiling answer you?
ABIGAIL: He has my heart; I smile against my will.
(*Aside*)
LODOWICK: Barabas, thou know'st I have lov'd thy daughter
    long.
BARABAS: And so has she done you, even from a child.
LODOWICK: And now I can no longer hold my mind.
BARABAS: Nor I the affection that I bear to you.
LODOWICK: This is thy diamond; tell me, shall I have it?
BARABAS: Win it, and wear it; it is yet unsoil'd.
    O, but I know your lordship would disdain
    To marry with the daughter of a Jew:

And yet I'll give her many a golden cross
With Christian posies round about the ring.

LODOWICK: 'Tis not thy wealth, but her that I esteem;
Yet crave I thy consent.

BARABAS: And mine you have; yet let me talk to her.—
This offspring of Cain, this Jebusite,
That never tasted of the Passover,
Nor e'er shall see the land of Canaan,
Nor our Messias that is yet to come;
This gentle maggot, Lodowick, I mean,
Must be deluded: let him have thy hand,
But keep thy heart till Don Mathias comes.

(*Aside to her*)

ABIGAIL: What, shall I be betroth'd to Lodowick?

BARABAS: It's no sin to deceive a Christian;
For they themselves hold it a principle,
Faith is not to be held with heretics:
But all are heretics that are not Jews;
This follows well, and therefore, daughter, fear not.—

(*Aside to her*)

I have entreated her, and she will grant.

LODOWICK: Then, gentle Abigail, plight thy faith to me.

ABIGAIL: I cannot choose, seeing my father bids:
Nothing but death shall part my love and me.

LODOWICK: Now have I that for which my soul hath long'd.

BARABAS: So have not I; but yet I hope I shall.

(*Aside*)

ABIGAIL: O wretched Abigail, what hast thou done?

(*Aside*)

LODOWICK: Why on the sudden is your colour chang'd?

ABIGAIL: I know not: but farewell; I must be gone.

BARABAS: Stay her, but let her not speak one word more.

LODOWICK: Mute o' the sudden! here's a sudden change.

BARABAS: O, muse not at it; 'tis the Hebrews' guise,
That maidens new-betroth'd should weep a while:
Trouble her not; sweet Lodowick, depart:
She is thy wife, and thou shalt be mine heir.

LODOWICK: O, is't the custom? then I am resolv'd:
But rather let the brightsome heavens be dim,

And nature's beauty choke with stifling clouds,
Than my fair Abigail should frown on me.—
There comes the villain; now I'll be reveng'd.

Re-enter MATHIAS.

BARABAS: Be quiet, Lodowick; it is enough
That I have made thee sure to Abigail.

LODOWICK: Well, let him go.

(*Exit*)

BARABAS: Well, but for me, as you went in at doors
You had been stabb'd: but not a word on't now;
Here must no speeches pass, nor swords be drawn.

MATHIAS: Suffer me, Barabas, but to follow him.

BARABAS: No; so shall I, if any hurt be done,
Be made an accessary of your deeds:
Revenge it on him when you meet him next.

MATHIAS: For this I'll have his heart.

BARABAS: Do so. Lo, here I give thee Abigail!

MATHIAS: What greater gift can poor Mathias have?
Shall Lodowick rob me of so fair a love?
My life is not so dear as Abigail.

BARABAS: My heart misgives me, that, to cross your love,
He's with your mother; therefore after him.

MATHIAS: What, is he gone unto my mother?

BARABAS: Nay, if you will, stay till she comes herself.

MATHIAS: I cannot stay; for, if my mother come,
She'll die with grief.

(*Exit*)

ABIGAIL: I cannot take my leave of him for tears.
Father, why have you thus incens'd them both?

BARABAS: What's that to thee?

ABIGAIL: I'll make 'em friends again.

BARABAS: You'll make 'em friends! are there not Jews enow in
Malta,
But thou must dote upon a Christian?

ABIGAIL: I will have Don Mathias; he is my love.

BARABAS: Yes, you shall have him.—Go, put her in.

ITHAMORE: Ay, I'll put her in.

(*Puts in* ABIGAIL)

BARABAS: Now tell me, Ithamore, how lik'st thou this?

ITHAMORE: Faith, master, I think by this
  You purchase both their lives: is it not so?
BARABAS: True; and it shall be cunningly perform'd.
ITHAMORE: O, master, that I might have a hand in this!
BARABAS: Ay, so thou shalt; 'tis thou must do the deed:
  Take this, and bear it to Mathias straight,
(*Giving a letter*)
  And tell him that it comes from Lodowick.
ITHAMORE: 'Tis poison'd, is it not?
BARABAS: No, no; and yet it might be done that way:
  It is a challenge feign'd from Lodowick.
ITHAMORE: Fear not; I will so set his heart a-fire,
  That he shall verily think it comes from him.
BARABAS: I cannot choose but like thy readiness:
  Yet be not rash, but do it cunningly.
ITHAMORE: As I behave myself in this, employ me hereafter.
BARABAS: Away, then!
(*Exit* ITHAMORE)
  So; now will I go in to Lodowick,
  And, like a cunning spirit, feign some lie,
  Till I have set 'em both at enmity.
(*Exit*)

Act III

Enter BELLAMIRA.

BELLAMIRA: Since this town was besieg'd, my gain grows cold:
    The time has been, that but for one bare night
    A hundred ducats have been freely given;
    But now against my will I must be chaste:
    And yet I know my beauty doth not fail.
    From Venice merchants, and from Padua
    Were wont to come rare-witted gentlemen,
    Scholars I mean, learned and liberal;
    And now, save Pilia-Borza, comes there none,
    And he is very seldom from my house;
    And here he comes.

Enter PILIA-BORZA.

PILIA-BORZA: Hold thee, wench, there's something for thee to spend.

(*Shewing a bag of silver*)

BELLAMIRA: 'Tis silver; I disdain it.

PILIA-BORZA: Ay, but the Jew has gold,
    And I will have it, or it shall go hard.

BELLAMIRA: Tell me, how cam'st thou by this?

PILIA-BORZA: Faith, walking the back-lanes, through the gardens, I
    chanced to cast mine eye up to the Jew's counting-house, where I
    saw some bags of money, and in the night I clambered up with my
    hooks; and, as I was taking my choice, I heard a rumbling in the
    house; so I took only this, and run my way.—But here's the Jew's
    man.

BELLAMIRA: Hide the bag.

Enter ITHAMORE.

PILIA-BORZA: Look not towards him, let's away. Zoons, what a
    looking thou keepest! thou'lt betray's anon.

(*Exeunt* BELLAMIRA *and* PILIA-BORZA)

ITHAMORE: O, the sweetest face that ever I beheld! I know she is a
    courtezan by her attire: now would I give a hundred of the Jew's
    crowns that I had such a concubine.
    Well, I have deliver'd the challenge in such sort,
    As meet they will, and fighting die,—brave sport!

(*Exit*)

Enter MATHIAS.

MATHIAS: This is the place: now Abigail shall see
    Whether Mathias holds her dear or no.

Enter LODOWICK.

    What, dares the villain write in such base terms?

(*Looking at a letter*)

LODOWICK: I did it; and revenge it, if thou dar'st!

(*They fight*)

Enter BARABAS *above.*

BARABAS: O, bravely fought! and yet they thrust not home.
    Now, Lodovico! now, Mathias!—So;

(*Both fall*)

    So, now they have shew'd themselves to be tall fellows.
    (*Cries within*) Part 'em, part 'em!

BARABAS: Ay, part 'em now they are dead. Farewell, farewell!

(*Exit above*)

Enter FERNEZE, KATHARINE, *and* ATTENDANTS.

FERNEZE: What sight is this! my Lodovico slain!
    These arms of mine shall be thy sepulchre.

KATHARINE: Who is this? my son Mathias slain!

FERNEZE: O Lodowick, hadst thou perish'd by the Turk,
    Wretched Ferneze might have veng'd thy death!

KATHARINE: Thy son slew mine, and I'll revenge his death.

FERNEZE: Look, Katharine, look! thy son gave mine these
    wounds.

KATHARINE: O, leave to grieve me! I am griev'd enough.

FERNEZE: O, that my sighs could turn to lively breath,
    And these my tears to blood, that he might live!

KATHARINE: Who made them enemies?

FERNEZE: I know not; and that grieves me most of all.

KATHARINE: My son lov'd thine.

FERNEZE: And so did Lodowick him.

KATHARINE: Lend me that weapon that did kill my son,
    And it shall murder me.

FERNEZE: Nay, madam, stay; that weapon was my son's,
    And on that rather should Ferneze die.

KATHARINE: Hold; let's inquire the causers of their deaths,
    That we may venge their blood upon their heads.

FERNEZE: Then take them up, and let them be interr'd
	Within one sacred monument of stone;
	Upon which altar I will offer up
	My daily sacrifice of sighs and tears,
	And with my prayers pierce impartial heavens,
	Till they (*reveal*) the causers of our smarts,
	Which forc'd their hands divide united hearts.
	Come, Katharine; our losses equal are;
	Then of true grief let us take equal share.
(*Exeunt with the bodies*)
Enter ITHAMORE.
ITHAMORE: Why, was there ever seen such villany,
	So neatly plotted, and so well perform'd?
	Both held in hand, and flatly both beguil'd?
Enter ABIGAIL.
ABIGAIL: Why, how now, Ithamore! why laugh'st thou so?
ITHAMORE: O mistress! ha, ha, ha!
ABIGAIL: Why, what ail'st thou?
ITHAMORE: O, my master!
ABIGAIL: Ha!
ITHAMORE: O mistress, I have the bravest, gravest, secret, subtle,
	bottle-nosed knave to my master, that ever gentleman had!
ABIGAIL: Say, knave, why rail'st upon my father thus?
ITHAMORE: O, my master has the bravest policy!
ABIGAIL: Wherein?
ITHAMORE: Why, know you not?
ABIGAIL: Why, no.
ITHAMORE: Know you not of Mathia(s') and Don Lodowick('s)
	disaster?
ABIGAIL: No: what was it?
ITHAMORE: Why, the devil inverted a challenge, my master writ
	it, and I carried it, first to Lodowick, and imprimis to
	Mathia(s);
	And then they met, (*and*), as the story says,
	In doleful wise they ended both their days.
ABIGAIL: And was my father furtherer of their deaths?
ITHAMORE: Am I Ithamore?
ABIGAIL: Yes.
ITHAMORE: So sure did your father write, and I carry the challenge.

ABIGAIL: Well, Ithamore, let me request thee this;
    Go to the new-made nunnery, and inquire
    For any of the friars of Saint Jaques,
    And say, I pray them come and speak with me.
ITHAMORE: I pray, mistress, will you answer me to one question?
ABIGAIL: Well, sirrah, what is't?
ITHAMORE: A very feeling one: have not the nuns fine sport with the
    friars now and then?
ABIGAIL: Go to, Sirrah Sauce! is this your question? get ye gone.
ITHAMORE: I will, forsooth, mistress.
(*Exit*)
ABIGAIL: Hard-hearted father, unkind Barabas!
    Was this the pursuit of thy policy,
    To make me shew them favour severally,
    That by my favour they should both be slain?
    Admit thou lov'dst not Lodowick for his sire,
    Yet Don Mathias ne'er offended thee:
    But thou wert set upon extreme revenge,
    Because the prior dispossess'd thee once,
    And couldst not venge it but upon his son;
    Nor on his son but by Mathias' means;
    Nor on Mathias but by murdering me:
    But I perceive there is no love on earth,
    Pity in Jews, nor piety in Turks.—
    But here comes cursed Ithamore with the friar.
Re-enter ITHAMORE *with* FRIAR JACOMO.
FRIAR JACOMO: Virgo, salve.
ITHAMORE: When duck you?
ABIGAIL: Welcome, grave friar.—Ithamore, be gone.
(*Exit* ITHAMORE)
    Know, holy sir, I am bold to solicit thee.
FRIAR JACOMO: Wherein?
ABIGAIL: To get me be admitted for a nun.
FRIAR JACOMO: Why, Abigail, it is not yet long since
    That I did labour thy admission,
    And then thou didst not like that holy life.
ABIGAIL: Then were my thoughts so frail and unconfirm'd
    As I was chain'd to follies of the world:
    But now experience, purchased with grief,

Has made me see the difference of things.
My sinful soul, alas, hath pac'd too long
The fatal labyrinth of misbelief,
Far from the sun that gives eternal life!

FRIAR JACOMO: Who taught thee this?

ABIGAIL: The abbess of the house,
Whose zealous admonition I embrace:
O, therefore, Jacomo, let me be one,
Although unworthy, of that sisterhood!

FRIAR JACOMO: Abigail, I will: but see thou change no more,
For that will be most heavy to thy soul.

ABIGAIL: That was my father's fault.

FRIAR JACOMO: Thy father's! how?

ABIGAIL: Nay, you shall pardon me.—O Barabas,
Though thou deservest hardly at my hands,
Yet never shall these lips bewray thy life!

(*Aside*)

FRIAR JACOMO: Come, shall we go?

ABIGAIL: My duty waits on you.

(*Exeunt*)

Enter BARABAS, *reading a letter.*

BARABAS: What, Abigail become a nun again!
False and unkind! what, hast thou lost thy father?
And, all unknown and unconstrain'd of me,
Art thou again got to the nunnery?
Now here she writes, and wills me to repent:
Repentance! Spurca! what pretendeth this?
I fear she knows—'tis so—of my device
In Don Mathias' and Lodovico's deaths:
If so, 'tis time that it be seen into;
For she that varies from me in belief,
Gives great presumption that she loves me not,
Or, loving, doth dislike of something done.—
But who comes here?

Enter ITHAMORE.

O Ithamore, come near;
Come near, my love; come near, thy master's life,
My trusty servant, nay, my second self;
For I have now no hope but even in thee,

CHRISTOPHER MARLOWE

And on that hope my happiness is built.
When saw'st thou Abigail?

ITHAMORE: To-day.

BARABAS: With whom?

ITHAMORE: A friar.

BARABAS: A friar! false villain, he hath done the deed.

ITHAMORE: How, sir!

BARABAS: Why, made mine Abigail a nun.

ITHAMORE: That's no lie; for she sent me for him.

BARABAS: O unhappy day!
False, credulous, inconstant Abigail!
But let 'em go: and, Ithamore, from hence
Ne'er shall she grieve me more with her disgrace;
Ne'er shall she live to inherit aught of mine,
Be bless'd of me, nor come within my gates,
But perish underneath my bitter curse,
Like Cain by Adam for his brother's death.

ITHAMORE: O master—

BARABAS: Ithamore, entreat not for her; I am mov'd,
And she is hateful to my soul and me:
And, 'less thou yield to this that I entreat,
I cannot think but that thou hat'st my life.

ITHAMORE: Who, I, master? why, I'll run to some rock,
And throw myself headlong into the sea;
Why, I'll do any thing for your sweet sake.

BARABAS: O trusty Ithamore! no servant, but my friend!
I here adopt thee for mine only heir:
All that I have is thine when I am dead;
And, whilst I live, use half; spend as myself;
Here, take my keys,—I'll give 'em thee anon;
Go buy thee garments; but thou shalt not want:
Only know this, that thus thou art to do—
But first go fetch me in the pot of rice
That for our supper stands upon the fire.

ITHAMORE: I hold my head, my master's hungry (*Aside*)—I go, sir.
(*Exit*)

BARABAS: Thus every villain ambles after wealth,
Although he ne'er be richer than in hope:—
But, husht!

Re-enter ITHAMORE *with the pot.*

ITHAMORE: Here 'tis, master.

BARABAS: Well said, Ithamore! What, hast thou brought
    The ladle with thee too?

ITHAMORE: Yes, sir; the proverb says, he that eats with the devil had
    need of a long spoon; I have brought you a ladle.

BARABAS: Very well, Ithamore; then now be secret;
    And, for thy sake, whom I so dearly love,
    Now shalt thou see the death of Abigail,
    That thou mayst freely live to be my heir.

ITHAMORE: Why, master, will you poison her with a mess of rice-
    porridge? that will preserve life, make her round and plump, and
    batten more than you are aware.

BARABAS: Ay, but, Ithamore, seest thou this?
    It is a precious powder that I bought
    Of an Italian, in Ancona, once,
    Whose operation is to bind, infect,
    And poison deeply, yet not appear
    In forty hours after it is ta'en.

ITHAMORE: How, master?

BARABAS: Thus, Ithamore:
    This even they use in Malta here,—'tis call'd
    Saint Jaques' Even,—and then, I say, they use
    To send their alms unto the nunneries:
    Among the rest, bear this, and set it there:
    There's a dark entry where they take it in,
    Where they must neither see the messenger,
    Nor make inquiry who hath sent it them.

ITHAMORE: How so?

BARABAS: Belike there is some ceremony in't.
    There, Ithamore, must thou go place this pot:
    Stay; let me spice it first.

ITHAMORE: Pray, do, and let me help you, master.
    Pray, let me taste first.

BARABAS: Prithee, do. (ITHAMORE *tastes*) What say'st thou now?

ITHAMORE: Troth, master, I'm loath such a pot of pottage should be
    spoiled.

BARABAS: Peace, Ithamore! 'tis better so than spar'd.

(*Puts the powder into the pot*)

Assure thyself thou shalt have broth by the eye:
My purse, my coffer, and myself is thine.

ITHAMORE: Well, master, I go.

BARABAS: Stay; first let me stir it, Ithamore.
As fatal be it to her as the draught
Of which great Alexander drunk, and died;
And with her let it work like Borgia's wine,
Whereof his sire the Pope was poisoned!
In few, the blood of Hydra, Lerna's bane,
The juice of hebon, and Cocytus' breath,
And all the poisons of the Stygian pool,
Break from the fiery kingdom, and in this
Vomit your venom, and envenom her
That, like a fiend, hath left her father thus!

ITHAMORE: What a blessing has he given't! was ever pot of rice-
porridge so sauced? (*Aside*)—What shall I do with it?

BARABAS: O my sweet Ithamore, go set it down;
And come again so soon as thou hast done,
For I have other business for thee.

ITHAMORE: Here's a drench to poison a whole stable of Flanders
mares: I'll carry't to the nuns with a powder.

BARABAS: And the horse-pestilence to boot: away!

ITHAMORE: I am gone:
Pay me my wages, for my work is done.

(*Exit with the pot*)

BARABAS: I'll pay thee with a vengeance, Ithamore!

(*Exit*)

Enter FERNEZE, MARTIN DEL BOSCO, KNIGHTS, *and* BASSO.

FERNEZE: Welcome, great basso: how fares Calymath?
What wind drives you thus into Malta-road?

BASSO: The wind that bloweth all the world besides,
Desire of gold.

FERNEZE: Desire of gold, great sir!
That's to be gotten in the Western Inde:
In Malta are no golden minerals.

BASSO: To you of Malta thus saith Calymath:
The time you took for respite is at hand
For the performance of your promise pass'd;
And for the tribute-money I am sent.

FERNEZE: Basso, in brief, shalt have no tribute here,
 Nor shall the heathens live upon our spoil:
 First will we raze the city-walls ourselves,
 Lay waste the island, hew the temples down,
 And, shipping off our goods to Sicily,
 Open an entrance for the wasteful sea,
 Whose billows, beating the resistless banks,
 Shall overflow it with their refluence.

BASSO: Well, governor, since thou hast broke the league
 By flat denial of the promis'd tribute,
 Talk not of razing down your city-walls;
 You shall not need trouble yourselves so far,
 For Selim Calymath shall come himself,
 And with brass bullets batter down your towers,
 And turn proud Malta to a wilderness,
 For these intolerable wrongs of yours:
 And so, farewell.

FERNEZE: Farewell.

(*Exit* BASSO)

 And now, you men of Malta, look about,
 And let's provide to welcome Calymath:
 Close your port-cullis, charge your basilisks,
 And, as you profitably take up arms,
 So now courageously encounter them,
 For by this answer broken is the league,
 And naught is to be look'd for now but wars,
 And naught to us more welcome is than wars.

(*Exeunt*)

Enter FRIAR JACOMO *and* FRIAR BARNARDINE.

FRIAR JACOMO: O brother, brother, all the nuns are sick,
 And physic will not help them! they must die.

FRIAR BARNARDINE: The abbess sent for me to be
 confess'd:
 O, what a sad confession will there be!

FRIAR JACOMO: And so did fair Maria send for me:
 I'll to her lodging; hereabouts she lies.

(*Exit*)

Enter ABIGAIL.

FRIAR BARNARDINE: What, all dead, save only Abigail!

ABIGAIL: And I shall die too, for I feel death coming.
   Where is the friar that convers'd with me?
FRIAR BARNARDINE: O, he is gone to see the other nuns.
ABIGAIL: I sent for him; but, seeing you are come,
   Be you my ghostly father: and first know,
   That in this house I liv'd religiously,
   Chaste, and devout, much sorrowing for my sins;
   But, ere I came—
FRIAR BARNARDINE: What then?
ABIGAIL: I did offend high heaven so grievously
   As I am almost desperate for my sins;
   And one offense torments me more than all.
   You knew Mathias and Don Lodowick?
FRIAR BARNARDINE: Yes; what of them?
ABIGAIL: My father did contract me to 'em both;
   First to Don Lodowick: him I never lov'd;
   Mathias was the man that I held dear,
   And for his sake did I become a nun.
FRIAR BARNARDINE: So: say how was their end?
ABIGAIL: Both, jealous of my love, envied each other;
   And by my father's practice, which is there
(*Gives writing*)
   Set down at large, the gallants were both slain.
FRIAR BARNARDINE: O, monstrous villany!
ABIGAIL: To work my peace, this I confess to thee:
   Reveal it not; for then my father dies.
FRIAR BARNARDINE: Know that confession must not be reveal'd;
   The canon-law forbids it, and the priest
   That makes it known, being degraded first,
   Shall be condemn'd, and then sent to the fire.
ABIGAIL: So I have heard; pray, therefore, keep it close.
   Death seizeth on my heart: ah, gentle friar,
   Convert my father that he may be sav'd,
   And witness that I die a Christian!
(*Dies*)
FRIAR BARNARDINE: Ay, and a virgin too; that grieves me most.
   But I must to the Jew, and exclaim on him,
   And make him stand in fear of me.
Re-enter FRIAR JACOMO.

FRIAR JACOMO: O brother, all the nuns are dead! let's bury them.

FRIAR BARNARDINE: First help to bury this; then go with me,
And help me to exclaim against the Jew.

FRIAR JACOMO: Why, what has he done?

FRIAR BARNARDINE: A thing that makes me tremble to unfold.

FRIAR JACOMO: What, has he crucified a child?

FRIAR BARNARDINE: No, but a worse thing: 'twas told me in shrift;
Thou know'st 'tis death, an if it be reveal'd.

Come, let's away.

(*Exeunt*)

Act IV

Enter BARABAS *and* ITHAMORE. *Bells within.*

BARABAS: There is no music to a Christian's knell:
How sweet the bells ring, now the nuns are dead,
That sound at other times like tinkers' pans!
I was afraid the poison had not wrought,
Or, though it wrought, it would have done no good,
For every year they swell, and yet they live:
Now all are dead, not one remains alive.
ITHAMORE: That's brave, master: but think you it will not be known?
BARABAS: How can it, if we two be secret?
ITHAMORE: For my part, fear you not.
BARABAS: I'd cut thy throat, if I did.
ITHAMORE: And reason too.
But here's a royal monastery hard by;
Good master, let me poison all the monks.
BARABAS: Thou shalt not need; for, now the nuns are dead,
They'll die with grief.
ITHAMORE: Do you not sorrow for your daughter's death?
BARABAS: No, but I grieve because she liv'd so long,
An Hebrew born, and would become a Christian:
Cazzo, diabolo!
ITHAMORE: Look, look, master; here come two religious caterpillars.
Enter FRIAR JACOMO *and* FRIAR BARNARDINE.
BARABAS: I smelt 'em ere they came.
ITHAMORE: God-a-mercy, nose! Come, let's begone.
FRIAR BARNARDINE: Stay, wicked Jew; repent, I say, and stay.
FRIAR JACOMO: Thou hast offended, therefore must be damn'd.
BARABAS: I fear they know we sent the poison'd broth.
ITHAMORE: And so do I, master; therefore speak 'em fair.
FRIAR BARNARDINE: Barabas, thou hast—
FRIAR JACOMO: Ay, that thou hast—
BARABAS: True, I have money; what though I have?
FRIAR BARNARDINE: Thou art a—
FRIAR JACOMO: Ay, that thou art, a—
BARABAS: What needs all this? I know I am a Jew.

FRIAR BARNARDINE: Thy daughter—

FRIAR JACOMO: Ay, thy daughter—

BARABAS: O, speak not of her! then I die with grief.

FRIAR BARNARDINE: Remember that—

FRIAR JACOMO: Ay, remember that—

BARABAS: I must needs say that I have been a great usurer.

FRIAR BARNARDINE: Thou hast committed—

BARABAS: Fornication: but that was in another country;
    And besides, the wench is dead.

FRIAR BARNARDINE: Ay, but, Barabas,
    Remember Mathias and Don Lodowick.

BARABAS: Why, what of them?

FRIAR BARNARDINE: I will not say that by a forged challenge
    they met.

BARABAS: She has confess'd, and we are both undone,
    My bosom inmate! but I must dissemble.—

(*Aside to* ITHAMORE)

    O holy friars, the burden of my sins
    Lie heavy on my soul! then, pray you, tell me,
    Is't not too late now to turn Christian?
    I have been zealous in the Jewish faith,
    Hard-hearted to the poor, a covetous wretch,
    That would for lucre's sake have sold my soul;
    A hundred for a hundred I have ta'en;
    And now for store of wealth may I compare
    With all the Jews in Malta: but what is wealth?
    I am a Jew, and therefore am I lost.
    Would penance serve (*to atone*) for this my sin,
    I could afford to whip myself to death,—

ITHAMORE: And so could I; but penance will not serve.

BARABAS: To fast, to pray, and wear a shirt of hair,
    And on my knees creep to Jerusalem.
    Cellars of wine, and sollars full of wheat,
    Warehouses stuff'd with spices and with drugs,
    Whole chests of gold in bullion and in coin,
    Besides, I know not how much weight in pearl
    Orient and round, have I within my house;
    At Alexandria merchandise untold;
    But yesterday two ships went from this town,

Their voyage will be worth ten thousand crowns;
In Florence, Venice, Antwerp, London, Seville,
Frankfort, Lubeck, Moscow, and where not,
Have I debts owing; and, in most of these,
Great sums of money lying in the banco;
All this I'll give to some religious house,
So I may be baptiz'd, and live therein.

FRIAR JACOMO: O good Barabas, come to our house!

FRIAR BARNARDINE: O, no, good Barabas, come to our house!
And, Barabas, you know—

BARABAS: I know that I have highly sinn'd:
You shall convert me, you shall have all my wealth.

FRIAR JACOMO: O Barabas, their laws are strict!

BARABAS: I know they are; and I will be with you.

FRIAR BARNARDINE: They wear no shirts, and they go bare-foot
too.

BARABAS: Then 'tis not for me; and I am resolv'd
You shall confess me, and have all my goods.

FRIAR JACOMO: Good Barabas, come to me.

BARABAS: You see I answer him, and yet he stays;
Rid him away, and go you home with me.

FRIAR JACOMO: I'll be with you to-night.

BARABAS: Come to my house at one o'clock this night.

FRIAR JACOMO: You hear your answer, and you may be gone.

FRIAR BARNARDINE: Why, go, get you away.

FRIAR JACOMO: I will not go for thee.

FRIAR BARNARDINE: Not! then I'll make thee go.

FRIAR JACOMO: How! dost call me rogue?

(*They fight*)

ITHAMORE: Part 'em, master, part 'em.

BARABAS: This is mere frailty: brethren, be content.—
Friar Barnardine, go you with Ithamore:
You know my mind; let me alone with him.

FRIAR JACOMO: Why does he go to thy house? let him be
gone.

BARABAS: I'll give him something, and so stop his mouth.

(*Exit* ITHAMORE *with Friar* BARNARDINE)
I never heard of any man but he
Malign'd the order of the Jacobins:

But do you think that I believe his words?
Why, brother, you converted Abigail;
And I am bound in charity to requite it,
And so I will. O Jacomo, fail not, but come.

FRIAR JACOMO: But, Barabas, who shall be your godfathers?
For presently you shall be shriv'd.

BARABAS: Marry, the Turk shall be one of my godfathers,
But not a word to any of your covent.

FRIAR JACOMO: I warrant thee, Barabas.

(*Exit*)

BARABAS: So, now the fear is past, and I am safe;
For he that shriv'd her is within my house:
What, if I murder'd him ere Jacomo comes?
Now I have such a plot for both their lives,
As never Jew nor Christian knew the like:
One turn'd my daughter, therefore he shall die;
The other knows enough to have my life,
Therefore 'tis not requisite he should live.
But are not both these wise men, to suppose
That I will leave my house, my goods, and all,
To fast and be well whipt? I'll none of that.
Now, Friar Barnardine, I come to you:
I'll feast you, lodge you, give you fair words,
And, after that, I and my trusty Turk—
No more, but so: it must and shall be done.

Enter ITHAMORE.

Ithamore, tell me, is the friar asleep?

ITHAMORE: Yes; and I know not what the reason is,
Do what I can, he will not strip himself,
Nor go to bed, but sleeps in his own clothes:
I fear me he mistrusts what we intend.

BARABAS: No; 'tis an order which the friars use:
Yet, if he knew our meanings, could he scape?

ITHAMORE: No, none can hear him, cry he ne'er so loud.

BARABAS: Why, true; therefore did I place him there:
The other chambers open towards the street.

ITHAMORE: You loiter, master; wherefore stay we thus?
O, how I long to see him shake his heels!

BARABAS: Come on, sirrah: Off with your girdle; make a handsome
     noose.—

(ITHAMORE *takes off his girdle, and ties a noose on it*)
     Friar, awake!

(*They put the noose round the* FRIAR'S *neck*)

FRIAR BARNARDINE: What, do you mean to strangle me?

ITHAMORE: Yes, 'cause you use to confess.

BARABAS: Blame not us, but the proverb,—Confess and be hanged.—
     Pull hard.

FRIAR BARNARDINE: What, will you have my life?

BARABAS: Pull hard, I say.—You would have had my goods.

ITHAMORE: Ay, and our lives too:—therefore pull amain.

(*They strangle the* FRIAR)
     'Tis neatly done, sir; here's no print at all.

BARABAS: Then is it as it should be. Take him up.

ITHAMORE: Nay, master, be ruled by me a little. (*Takes the body, sets it
     upright against the wall, and puts a staff in its hand*) So, let him lean
     upon his staff; excellent! he stands as if he were begging of bacon.

BARABAS: Who would not think but that this friar liv'd?
     What time o' night is't now, sweet Ithamore?

ITHAMORE: Towards one.

BARABAS: Then will not Jacomo be long from hence.

(*Exeunt*)

Enter FRIAR JACOMO.

FRIAR JACOMO: This is the hour wherein I shall proceed;
     O happy hour, wherein I shall convert
     An infidel, and bring his gold into our treasury!
     But soft! is not this Barnardine? it is;
     And, understanding I should come this way,
     Stands here o' purpose, meaning me some wrong,
     And intercept my going to the Jew.—
     Barnardine!
     Wilt thou not speak? thou think'st I see thee not;
     Away, I'd wish thee, and let me go by:
     No, wilt thou not? nay, then, I'll force my way;
     And, see, a staff stands ready for the purpose.
     As thou lik'st that, stop me another time!

(*Takes the staff, and strikes down the body*)

Enter BARABAS *and* ITHAMORE.

BARABAS: Why, how now, Jacomo! what hast thou done?

FRIAR JACOMO: Why, stricken him that would have struck at me.

BARABAS: Who is it? Barnardine! now, out, alas, he is slain!

ITHAMORE: Ay, master, he's slain; look how his brains drop out on's nose.

FRIAR JACOMO: Good sirs, I have done't: but nobody knows it but you
    two; I may escape.

BARABAS: So might my man and I hang with you for company.

ITHAMORE: No; let us bear him to the magistrates.

FRIAR JACOMO: Good Barabas, let me go.

BARABAS: No, pardon me; the law must have his course:
    I must be forc'd to give in evidence,
    That, being importun'd by this Barnardine
    To be a Christian, I shut him out,
    And there he sate: now I, to keep my word,
    And give my goods and substance to your house,
    Was up thus early, with intent to go
    Unto your friary, because you stay'd.

ITHAMORE: Fie upon 'em! master, will you turn Christian, when holy
    friars turn devils and murder one another?

BARABAS: No; for this example I'll remain a Jew:
    Heaven bless me! what, a friar a murderer!
    When shall you see a Jew commit the like?

ITHAMORE: Why, a Turk could ha' done no more.

BARABAS: To-morrow is the sessions; you shall to it.—
    Come, Ithamore, let's help to take him hence.

FRIAR JACOMO: Villains, I am a sacred person; touch me not.

BARABAS: The law shall touch you; we'll but lead you, we:
    'Las, I could weep at your calamity!—
    Take in the staff too, for that must be shown:
    Law wills that each particular be known.

(*Exeunt*)

Enter BELLAMIRA *and* PILIA-BORZA.

BELLAMIRA: Pilia-Borza, didst thou meet with Ithamore?

PILIA-BORZA: I did.

BELLAMIRA: And didst thou deliver my letter?

PILIA-BORZA: I did.

BELLAMIRA: And what thinkest thou? will he come?

PILIA-BORZA: I think so: and yet I cannot tell; for, at the reading of
    the letter, he looked like a man of another world.

             CHRISTOPHER MARLOWE

BELLAMIRA: Why so?

PILIA-BORZA: That such a base slave as he should be saluted by such a tall man as I am, from such a beautiful dame as you.

BELLAMIRA: And what said he?

PILIA-BORZA: Not a wise word; only gave me a nod, as who should say, "Is it even so?" and so I left him, being driven to a non-plus at the critical aspect of my terrible countenance.

BELLAMIRA: And where didst meet him?

PILIA-BORZA: Upon mine own free-hold, within forty foot of the gallows, conning his neck-verse, I take it, looking of a friar's execution; whom I saluted with an old hempen proverb, Hodie tibi, cras mihi, and so I left him to the mercy of the hangman: but, the exercise being done, see where he comes.

Enter ITHAMORE.

ITHAMORE: I never knew a man take his death so patiently as this friar; he was ready to leap off ere the halter was about his neck; and, when the hangman had put on his hempen tippet, he made such haste to his prayers, as if he had had another cure to serve. Well, go whither he will, I'll be none of his followers in haste: and, now I think on't, going to the execution, a fellow met me with a muschatoes like a raven's wing, and a dagger with a hilt like a warming-pan; and he gave me a letter from one Madam Bellamira, saluting me in such sort as if he had meant to make clean my boots with his lips; the effect was, that I should come to her house: I wonder what the reason is; it may be she sees more in me than I can find in myself; for she writes further, that she loves me ever since she saw me; and who would not requite such love? Here's her house; and here she comes; and now would I were gone! I am not worthy to look upon her.

PILIA-BORZA: This is the gentleman you writ to.

ITHAMORE: Gentleman! he flouts me: what gentry can be in a poor Turk of tenpence? I'll be gone.

(*Aside*)

BELLAMIRA: Is't not a sweet-faced youth, Pilia?

ITHAMORE: Again, sweet youth! (*Aside*)—Did not you, sir, bring the sweet youth a letter?

PILIA-BORZA: I did, sir, and from this gentlewoman, who, as myself and the rest of the family, stand or fall at your service.

BELLAMIRA: Though woman's modesty should hale me back,
    I can withhold no longer: welcome, sweet love.

ITHAMORE: Now am I clean, or rather foully, out of the way.
(*Aside*)
BELLAMIRA: Whither so soon?
ITHAMORE: I'll go steal some money from my master to make
    me handsome (*Aside*)—Pray, pardon me; I must go see a ship
    discharged.
BELLAMIRA: Canst thou be so unkind to leave me thus?
PILIA-BORZA: An ye did but know how she loves you, sir!
ITHAMORE: Nay, I care not how much she loves me.—Sweet
    Bellamira, would I had my master's wealth for thy sake!
PILIA-BORZA: And you can have it, sir, an if you please.
ITHAMORE: If 'twere above ground, I could, and would have it; but he
    hides and buries it up, as partridges do their eggs, under the earth.
PILIA-BORZA: And is't not possible to find it out?
ITHAMORE: By no means possible.
BELLAMIRA: What shall we do with this base villain, then?
(*Aside to* PILIA-BORZA)
PILIA-BORZA: Let me alone; do but you speak him fair.—
(*Aside to her*)
    But you know some secrets of the Jew,
    Which, if they were reveal'd, would do him harm.
ITHAMORE: Ay, and such as—go to, no more! I'll make him send me
    half he has, and glad he scapes so too: I'll write unto him; we'll
    have money straight.
PILIA-BORZA: Send for a hundred crowns at least.
ITHAMORE: Ten hundred thousand crowns.—(*writing*) MASTER
    BARABAS,—
PILIA-BORZA: Write not so submissively, but threatening him.
ITHAMORE: (*writing*) SIRRAH BARABAS, SEND ME A HUNDRED
    CROWNS.
PILIA-BORZA: Put in two hundred at least.
ITHAMORE: (*writing*) I CHARGE THEE SEND ME THREE HUNDRED BY
    THIS BEARER, AND THIS SHALL BE YOUR WARRANT: IF YOU DO
    NOT—NO MORE, BUT SO.
PILIA-BORZA: Tell him you will confess.
ITHAMORE: (*writing*) OTHERWISE I'LL CONFESS ALL.—
    Vanish, and return in a twinkle.
PILIA-BORZA: Let me alone; I'll use him in his kind.
ITHAMORE: Hang him, Jew!

CHRISTOPHER MARLOWE

(*Exit* PILIA-BORZA *with the letter*)

BELLAMIRA: Now, gentle Ithamore, lie in my lap.—
 Where are my maids? provide a cunning banquet;
 Send to the merchant, bid him bring me silks;
 Shall Ithamore, my love, go in such rags?

ITHAMORE: And bid the jeweller come hither too.

BELLAMIRA: I have no husband; sweet, I'll marry thee.

ITHAMORE: Content: but we will leave this paltry land,
 And sail from hence to Greece, to lovely Greece;—
 I'll be thy Jason, thou my golden fleece;—
 Where painted carpets o'er the meads are hurl'd,
 And Bacchus' vineyards overspread the world;
 Where woods and forests go in goodly green;—
 I'll be Adonis, thou shalt be Love's Queen;—
 The meads, the orchards, and the primrose-lanes,
 Instead of sedge and reed, bear sugar-canes:
 Thou in those groves, by Dis above,
 Shalt live with me, and be my love.

BELLAMIRA: Whither will I not go with gentle Ithamore?

Re-enter PILIA-BORZA.

ITHAMORE: How now! hast thou the gold (?)

PILIA-BORZA: Yes.

ITHAMORE: But came it freely? did the cow give down her milk freely?

PILIA-BORZA: At reading of the letter, he stared and stamped, and
 turned aside: I took him by the beard, and looked upon him thus;
 told him he were best to send it: then he hugged and embraced me.

ITHAMORE: Rather for fear than love.

PILIA-BORZA: Then, like a Jew, he laughed and jeered, and told me he
 loved me for your sake, and said what a faithful servant you had
 been.

ITHAMORE: The more villain he to keep me thus: here's goodly 'parel,
 is there not?

PILIA-BORZA: To conclude, he gave me ten crowns.

(*Delivers the money to* ITHAMORE)

ITHAMORE: But ten? I'll not leave him worth a grey groat. Give me a
 ream of paper: we'll have a kingdom of gold for't.

PILIA-BORZA: Write for five hundred crowns.

ITHAMORE: (*writing*) SIRRAH JEW, AS YOU LOVE YOUR LIFE,
 SEND ME

Five Hundred Crowns, And Give The Bearer A Hundred.—
   Tell him
   I must have't.

PILIA-BORZA: I warrant, your worship shall have't.

ITHAMORE: And, if he ask why I demand so much, tell him I scorn to
   write a line under a hundred crowns.

PILIA-BORZA: You'd make a rich poet, sir. I am gone.

(*Exit with the letter*)

ITHAMORE: Take thou the money; spend it for my sake.

BELLAMIRA: 'Tis not thy money, but thyself I weigh:
   Thus Bellamira esteems of gold;

(*Throws it aside*)

   But thus of thee.

(*Kisses him*)

ITHAMORE: That kiss again!—She runs division of my lips. What an
   eye she casts on me! it twinkles like a star.

(*Aside*)

BELLAMIRA: Come, my dear love, let's in and sleep together.

ITHAMORE: O, that ten thousand nights were put in one, that we
   might sleep seven years together afore we wake!

BELLAMIRA: Come, amorous wag, first banquet, and then
   sleep.

(*Exeunt*)

Enter BARABAS, *reading a letter.*

BARABAS: BARABAS, SEND ME THREE HUNDRED CROWNS;—
   Plain Barabas! O, that wicked courtezan!
   He was not wont to call me Barabas;—
   OR ELSE I WILL CONFESS;—ay, there it goes:
   But, if I get him, coupe de gorge for that.
   He sent a shaggy, tatter'd, staring slave,
   That, when he speaks, draws out his grisly beard,
   And winds it twice or thrice about his ear;
   Whose face has been a grind-stone for men's swords;
   His hands are hack'd, some fingers cut quite off;
   Who, when he speaks, grunts like a hog, and looks
   Like one that is employ'd in catzery
   And cross-biting; such a rogue
   As is the husband to a hundred whores;
   And I by him must send three hundred crowns.

Well, my hope is, he will not stay there still;
And, when he comes—O, that he were but here!

Enter Pilia-Borza.

Pilia-Borza: Jew, I must ha' more gold.

Barabas: Why, want'st thou any of thy tale?

Pilia-Borza: No; but three hundred will not serve his turn.

Barabas: Not serve his turn, sir!

Pilia-Borza: No, sir; and therefore I must have five hundred more.

Barabas: I'll rather——

Pilia-Borza: O, good words, sir, and send it you were best! see, there's his letter.

(*Gives letter*)

Barabas: Might he not as well come as send? pray, bid him come and fetch it: what he writes for you, ye shall have straight.

Pilia-Borza: Ay, and the rest too, or else——

Barabas: I must make this villain away (*Aside*)—Please you dine with me, sir—and you shall be most heartily poisoned.

(*Aside*)

Pilia-Borza: No, God-a-mercy. Shall I have these crowns?

Barabas: I cannot do it; I have lost my keys.

Pilia-Borza: O, if that be all, I can pick ope your locks.

Barabas: Or climb up to my counting-house window: you know my meaning.

Pilia-Borza: I know enough, and therefore talk not to me of your counting-house. The gold! or know, Jew, it is in my power to hang thee.

Barabas: I am betray'd.—

(*Aside*)

'Tis not five hundred crowns that I esteem;
I am not mov'd at that: this angers me,
That he, who knows I love him as myself,
Should write in this imperious vein. Why, sir,
You know I have no child, and unto whom
Should I leave all, but unto Ithamore?

Pilia-Borza: Here's many words, but no crowns: the crowns!

Barabas: Commend me to him, sir, most humbly,
And unto your good mistress as unknown.

Pilia-Borza: Speak, shall I have 'em, sir?

Barabas: Sir, here they are.—

(*Gives money*)

    O, that I should part with so much gold!—

(*Aside*)

    Here, take 'em, fellow, with as good a will——

    As I would see thee hang'd (*Aside*) O, love stops my breath!

    Never lov'd man servant as I do Ithamore.

PILIA-BORZA: I know it, sir.

BARABAS: Pray, when, sir, shall I see you at my house?

PILIA-BORZA: Soon enough to your cost, sir. Fare you well.

(*Exit*)

BARABAS: Nay, to thine own cost, villain, if thou com'st!

    Was ever Jew tormented as I am?

    To have a shag-rag knave to come (*force from me*)

    Three hundred crowns, and then five hundred crowns!

    Well; I must seek a means to rid 'em all,

    And presently; for in his villany

    He will tell all he knows, and I shall die for't.

    I have it:

    I will in some disguise go see the slave,

    And how the villain revels with my gold.

(*Exit*)

Enter BELLAMIRA, ITHAMORE, *and* PILIA-BORZA.

BELLAMIRA: I'll pledge thee, love, and therefore drink it off.

ITHAMORE: Say'st thou me so? have at it! and do you hear?

(*Whispers to her*)

BELLAMIRA: Go to, it shall be so.

ITHAMORE: Of that condition I will drink it up:

    Here's to thee.

BELLAMIRA: Nay, I'll have all or none.

ITHAMORE: There, if thou lov'st me, do not leave a drop.

BELLAMIRA: Love thee! fill me three glasses.

ITHAMORE: Three and fifty dozen: I'll pledge thee.

PILIA-BORZA: Knavely spoke, and like a knight-at-arms.

ITHAMORE: Hey, Rivo Castiliano! a man's a man.

BELLAMIRA: Now to the Jew.

ITHAMORE: Ha! to the Jew; and send me money he were best.

PILIA-BORZA: What wouldst thou do, if he should send thee none?

ITHAMORE: Do nothing: but I know what I know; he's a murderer.

BELLAMIRA: I had not thought he had been so brave a man.

    CHRISTOPHER MARLOWE

ITHAMORE: You knew Mathias and the governor's son; he and I killed
'em both, and yet never touched 'em.

PILIA-BORZA: O, bravely done!

ITHAMORE: I carried the broth that poisoned the nuns; and he and I,
snicle hand too fast, strangled a friar.

BELLAMIRA: You two alone?

ITHAMORE: We two; and 'twas never known, nor never shall be for me.

PILIA-BORZA: This shall with me unto the governor.
(*Aside to* BELLAMIRA)

BELLAMIRA: And fit it should: but first let's ha' more gold.—
(*Aside to* PILIA-BORZA)
Come, gentle Ithamore, lie in my lap.

ITHAMORE: Love me little, love me long: let music rumble,
Whilst I in thy incony lap do tumble.

Enter BARABAS, *disguised as a French musician, with a lute, and a nosegay
in his hat.*

BELLAMIRA: A French musician!—Come, let's hear your skill.

BARABAS: Must tuna my lute for sound, twang, twang, first.

ITHAMORE: Wilt drink, Frenchman? here's to thee with a—Pox on
this drunken hiccup!

BARABAS: Gramercy, monsieur.

BELLAMIRA: Prithee, Pilia-Borza, bid the fiddler give me the posy in
his hat there.

PILIA-BORZA: Sirrah, you must give my mistress your posy.

BARABAS: A votre commandement, madame.
(*Giving nosegay*)

BELLAMIRA: How sweet, my Ithamore, the flowers smell!

ITHAMORE: Like thy breath, sweetheart; no violet like 'em.

PILIA-BORZA: Foh! methinks they stink like a hollyhock.

BARABAS: So, now I am reveng'd upon 'em all:
The scent thereof was death; I poison'd it.
(*Aside*)

ITHAMORE: Play, fiddler, or I'll cut your cat's guts into chitterlings.

BARABAS: Pardonnez moi, be no in tune yet: so, now, now all be in.

ITHAMORE: Give him a crown, and fill me out more wine.

PILIA-BORZA: There's two crowns for thee: play.
(*Giving money*)

BARABAS: How liberally the villain gives me mine own gold!
(*Aside, and then plays*)

PILIA-BORZA: Methinks he fingers very well.

BARABAS: So did you when you stole my gold.
(*Aside*)

PILIA-BORZA: How swift he runs!

BARABAS: You run swifter when you threw my gold out of my window.
(*Aside*)

BELLAMIRA: Musician, hast been in Malta long?

BARABAS: Two, three, four month, madam.

ITHAMORE: Dost not know a Jew, one Barabas?

BARABAS: Very mush: monsieur, you no be his man?

PILIA-BORZA: His man!

ITHAMORE: I scorn the peasant: tell him so.

BARABAS: He knows it already.
(*Aside*)

ITHAMORE: 'Tis a strange thing of that Jew, he lives upon pickled grasshoppers and sauced mushrooms.

BARABAS: What a slave's this! the governor feeds not as I do.
(*Aside*)

ITHAMORE: He never put on clean shirt since he was circumcised.

BARABAS: O rascal! I change myself twice a-day.
(*Aside*)

ITHAMORE: The hat he wears, Judas left under the elder when he hanged himself.

BARABAS: 'Twas sent me for a present from the Great Cham.
(*Aside*)

PILIA-BORZA: A nasty slave he is.—Whither now, fiddler?

BARABAS: Pardonnez moi, monsieur; me be no well.

PILIA-BORZA: Farewell, fiddler (*Exit* BARABAS) One letter more to the Jew.

BELLAMIRA: Prithee, sweet love, one more, and write it sharp.

ITHAMORE: No, I'll send by word of mouth now.
   —Bid him deliver thee a thousand crowns, by the same token that the nuns loved rice, that Friar Barnardine slept in his own clothes; any of 'em will do it.

PILIA-BORZA: Let me alone to urge it, now I know the meaning.

ITHAMORE: The meaning has a meaning. Come, let's in:
   To undo a Jew is charity, and not sin.

(*Exeunt*)

Act V

Enter FERNEZE, KNIGHTS, MARTIN DEL BOSCO, *and* OFFICERS.

FERNEZE: Now, gentlemen, betake you to your arms,
And see that Malta be well fortified;
And it behoves you to be resolute;
For Calymath, having hover'd here so long,
Will win the town, or die before the walls.

FIRST KNIGHT: And die he shall; for we will never yield.

Enter BELLAMIRA *and* PILIA-BORZA.

BELLAMIRA: O, bring us to the governor!

FERNEZE: Away with her! she is a courtezan.

BELLAMIRA: Whate'er I am, yet, governor, hear me speak:
    I bring thee news by whom thy son was slain:
    Mathias did it not; it was the Jew.

PILIA-BORZA: Who, besides the slaughter of these gentlemen,
    Poison'd his own daughter and the nuns,
    Strangled a friar, and I know not what
    Mischief beside.

FERNEZE: Had we but proof of this——

BELLAMIRA: Strong proof, my lord: his man's now at my lodging,
    That was his agent; he'll confess it all.

FERNEZE: Go fetch him straight (*Exeunt* OFFICERS)
    I always fear'd that Jew.

Re-enter OFFICERS *with* BARABAS *and* ITHAMORE.

BARABAS: I'll go alone; dogs, do not hale me thus.

ITHAMORE: Nor me neither; I cannot out-run you, constable.—O, my
    belly!

BARABAS: One dram of powder more had made all sure:
    What a damn'd slave was I!

(*Aside*)

FERNEZE: Make fires, heat irons, let the rack be fetch'd.

FIRST KNIGHT: Nay, stay, my lord; 't may be he will confess.

BARABAS: Confess! what mean you, lords? who should confess?

FERNEZE: Thou and thy Turk; 'twas that slew my son.

ITHAMORE: Guilty, my lord, I confess. Your son and Mathias were
    both contracted unto Abigail: (*he*) forged a counterfeit challenge.

BARABAS: Who carried that challenge?

ITHAMORE: I carried it, I confess; but who writ it? marry, even he that strangled Barnardine, poisoned the nuns and his own daughter.

FERNEZE: Away with him! his sight is death to me.

BARABAS: For what, you men of Malta? hear me speak.
She is a courtezan, and he a thief,
And he my bondman: let me have law;
For none of this can prejudice my life.

FERNEZE: Once more, away with him!—You shall have law.

BARABAS: Devils, do your worst!—I('ll) live in spite of you.—
(*Aside*)
As these have spoke, so be it to their souls!—
I hope the poison'd flowers will work anon.
(*Aside*)
(*Exeunt* OFFICERS *with* BARABAS *and* ITHAMORE; BELLAMIRA, *and* PILIA-BORZA)
Enter KATHARINE.

KATHARINE: Was my Mathias murder'd by the Jew?
Ferneze, 'twas thy son that murder'd him.

FERNEZE: Be patient, gentle madam: it was he;
He forg'd the daring challenge made them fight.

KATHARINE: Where is the Jew? where is that murderer?

FERNEZE: In prison, till the law has pass'd on him.
Re-enter FIRST OFFICER.

FIRST OFFICER: My lord, the courtezan and her man are dead;
So is the Turk and Barabas the Jew.

FERNEZE: Dead!

FIRST OFFICER: Dead, my lord, and here they bring his body.

MARTIN DEL BOSCO: This sudden death of his is very strange.
Re-enter OFFICERS, *carrying* BARABAS *as dead.*

FERNEZE: Wonder not at it, sir; the heavens are just;
Their deaths were like their lives; then think not of 'em.—
Since they are dead, let them be buried:
For the Jew's body, throw that o'er the walls,
To be a prey for vultures and wild beasts.—
So, now away and fortify the town.
Exeunt all, leaving BARABAS *on the floor.*

BARABAS: (*rising*) What, all alone! well fare, sleepy drink!
I'll be reveng'd on this accursed town;

For by my means Calymath shall enter in:
I'll help to slay their children and their wives,
To fire the churches, pull their houses down,
Take my goods too, and seize upon my lands.
I hope to see the governor a slave,
And, rowing in a galley, whipt to death.

Enter CALYMATH, BASSOES, *and* TURKS.

CALYMATH: Whom have we there? a spy?

BARABAS: Yes, my good lord, one that can spy a place
Where you may enter, and surprize the town:
My name is Barabas; I am a Jew.

CALYMATH: Art thou that Jew whose goods we heard were sold
For tribute-money?

BARABAS: The very same, my lord:
And since that time they have hir'd a slave, my man,
To accuse me of a thousand villanies:
I was imprisoned, but scap (')d their hands.

CALYMATH: Didst break prison?

BARABAS: No, no: I drank of poppy and cold mandrake juice;
And being asleep, belike they thought me dead,
And threw me o'er the walls: so, or how else,
The Jew is here, and rests at your command.

CALYMATH: 'Twas bravely done: but tell me, Barabas,
Canst thou, as thou report'st, make Malta ours?

BARABAS: Fear not, my lord; for here, against the trench,
The rock is hollow, and of purpose digg'd,
To make a passage for the running streams
And common channels of the city.
Now, whilst you give assault unto the walls,
I'll lead five hundred soldiers through the vault,
And rise with them i' the middle of the town,
Open the gates for you to enter in;
And by this means the city is your own.

CALYMATH: If this be true, I'll make thee governor.

BARABAS: And, if it be not true, then let me die.

CALYMATH: Thou'st doom'd thyself.—Assault it presently.

(*Exeunt*)

Alarums within. Enter CALYMATH, BASSOES, TURKS, *and* BARABAS; *with*
FERNEZE *and* KNIGHTS *prisoners.*

CALYMATH: Now vail your pride, you captive Christians,
    And kneel for mercy to your conquering foe:
    Now where's the hope you had of haughty Spain?
    Ferneze, speak; had it not been much better
    To kept thy promise than be thus surpris'd?
FERNEZE: What should I say? we are captives, and must yield.
CALYMATH: Ay, villains, you must yield, and under Turkish yokes
    Shall groaning bear the burden of our ire:—
    And, Barabas, as erst we promis'd thee,
    For thy desert we make thee governor;
    Use them at thy discretion.
BARABAS: Thanks, my lord.
FERNEZE: O fatal day, to fall into the hands
    Of such a traitor and unhallow'd Jew!
    What greater misery could heaven inflict?
CALYMATH: 'Tis our command:—and, Barabas, we give,
    To guard thy person, these our Janizaries:
    Entreat them well, as we have used thee.—
    And now, brave bassoes, come; we'll walk about
    The ruin'd town, and see the wreck we made.—
    Farewell, brave Jew, farewell, great Barabas!
BARABAS: May all good fortune follow Calymath!
(*Exeunt* CALYMATH *and* BASSOES)
    And now, as entrance to our safety,
    To prison with the governor and these
    Captains, his consorts and confederates.
FERNEZE: O villain! heaven will be reveng'd on thee.
BARABAS: Away! no more; let him not trouble me.
(*Exeunt* TURKS *with* FERNEZE *and* KNIGHTS)
    Thus hast thou gotten, by thy policy,
    No simple place, no small authority:
    I now am governor of Malta; true,—
    But Malta hates me, and, in hating me,
    My life's in danger; and what boots it thee,
    Poor Barabas, to be the governor,
    Whenas thy life shall be at their command?
    No, Barabas, this must be look'd into;
    And, since by wrong thou gott'st authority,
    Maintain it bravely by firm policy;

At least, unprofitably lose it not;
For he that liveth in authority,
And neither gets him friends nor fills his bags,
Lives like the ass that Aesop speaketh of,
That labours with a load of bread and wine,
And leaves it off to snap on thistle-tops:
But Barabas will be more circumspect.
Begin betimes; Occasion's bald behind:
Slip not thine opportunity, for fear too late
Thou seek'st for much, but canst not compass it.—
Within here!

Enter FERNEZE, *with a* GUARD.

FERNEZE: My lord?

BARABAS: Ay, LORD; thus slaves will learn.
Now, governor,—stand by there, wait within,—

(*Exeunt* GUARD)

This is the reason that I sent for thee:
Thou seest thy life and Malta's happiness
Are at my arbitrement; and Barabas
At his discretion may dispose of both:
Now tell me, governor, and plainly too,
What think'st thou shall become of it and thee?

FERNEZE: This, Barabas; since things are in thy power,
I see no reason but of Malta's wreck,
Nor hope of thee but extreme cruelty:
Nor fear I death, nor will I flatter thee.

BARABAS: Governor, good words; be not so furious
'Tis not thy life which can avail me aught;
Yet you do live, and live for me you shall:
And as for Malta's ruin, think you not
'Twere slender policy for Barabas
To dispossess himself of such a place?
For sith, as once you said, within this isle,
In Malta here, that I have got my goods,
And in this city still have had success,
And now at length am grown your governor,
Yourselves shall see it shall not be forgot;
For, as a friend not known but in distress,
I'll rear up Malta, now remediless.

FERNEZE: Will Barabas recover Malta's loss?
    Will Barabas be good to Christians?
BARABAS: What wilt thou give me, governor, to procure
    A dissolution of the slavish bands
    Wherein the Turk hath yok'd your land and you?
    What will you give me if I render you
    The life of Calymath, surprise his men,
    And in an out-house of the city shut
    His soldiers, till I have consum'd 'em all with fire?
    What will you give him that procureth this?
FERNEZE: Do but bring this to pass which thou pretendest,
    Deal truly with us as thou intimatest,
    And I will send amongst the citizens,
    And by my letters privately procure
    Great sums of money for thy recompense:
    Nay, more, do this, and live thou governor still.
BARABAS: Nay, do thou this, Ferneze, and be free:
    Governor, I enlarge thee; live with me;
    Go walk about the city, see thy friends:
    Tush, send not letters to 'em; go thyself,
    And let me see what money thou canst make:
    Here is my hand that I'll set Malta free;
    And thus we cast it: to a solemn feast
    I will invite young Selim Calymath,
    Where be thou present, only to perform
    One stratagem that I'll impart to thee,
    Wherein no danger shall betide thy life,
    And I will warrant Malta free for ever.
FERNEZE: Here is my hand; believe me, Barabas,
    I will be there, and do as thou desirest.
    When is the time?
BARABAS: Governor, presently;
    For Calymath, when he hath view'd the town,
    Will take his leave, and sail toward Ottoman.
FERNEZE: Then will I, Barabas, about this coin,
    And bring it with me to thee in the evening.
BARABAS: Do so; but fail not: now farewell, Ferneze:—
(*Exit* FERNEZE)
    And thus far roundly goes the business:

Thus, loving neither, will I live with both,
Making a profit of my policy;
And he from whom my most advantage comes,
Shall be my friend.
This is the life we Jews are us'd to lead;
And reason too, for Christians do the like.
Well, now about effecting this device;
First, to surprise great Selim's soldiers,
And then to make provision for the feast,
That at one instant all things may be done:
My policy detests prevention.
To what event my secret purpose drives,
I know; and they shall witness with their lives.

(*Exeunt*)

Enter CALYMATH *and* BASSOES.

CALYMATH: Thus have we view'd the city, seen the sack,
And caus'd the ruins to be new-repair'd,
Which with our bombards' shot and basilisk(s)
We rent in sunder at our entry:
And, now I see the situation,
And how secure this conquer'd island stands,
Environ'd with the Mediterranean sea,
Strong-countermin'd with other petty isles,
And, toward Calabria, back'd by Sicily
(*Where Syracusian Dionysius reign'd*),
Two lofty turrets that command the town,
I wonder how it could be conquer'd thus.

Enter a MESSENGER.

MESSENGER: From Barabas, Malta's governor, I bring
A message unto mighty Calymath:
Hearing his sovereign was bound for sea,
To sail to Turkey, to great Ottoman,
He humbly would entreat your majesty
To come and see his homely citadel,
And banquet with him ere thou leav'st the isle.

CALYMATH: To banquet with him in his citadel!
I fear me, messenger, to feast my train
Within a town of war so lately pillag'd,
Will be too costly and too troublesome:

Yet would I gladly visit Barabas,
For well has Barabas deserv'd of us.

MESSENGER: Selim, for that, thus saith the governor,—
That he hath in (*his*) store a pearl so big,
So precious, and withal so orient,
As, be it valu'd but indifferently,
The price thereof will serve to entertain
Selim and all his soldiers for a month;
Therefore he humbly would entreat your highness
Not to depart till he has feasted you.

CALYMATH: I cannot feast my men in Malta-walls,
Except he place his tables in the streets.

MESSENGER: Know, Selim, that there is a monastery
Which standeth as an out-house to the town;
There will he banquet them; but thee at home,
With all thy bassoes and brave followers.

CALYMATH: Well, tell the governor we grant his suit;
We'll in this summer-evening feast with him.

MESSENGER: I shall, my lord.

(*Exit*)

CALYMATH: And now, bold bassoes, let us to our tents,
And meditate how we may grace us best,
To solemnize our governor's great feast.

(*Exeunt*)

Enter FERNEZE, KNIGHTS, *and* MARTIN DEL BOSCO.

FERNEZE: In this, my countrymen, be rul'd by me:
Have special care that no man sally forth
Till you shall hear a culverin discharg'd
By him that bears the linstock, kindled thus;
Then issue out and come to rescue me,
For happily I shall be in distress,
Or you released of this servitude.

FIRST KNIGHT: Rather than thus to live as Turkish thralls,
What will we not adventure?

FERNEZE: On, then; be gone.

KNIGHTS: Farewell, grave governor.

(*Exeunt, on one side,* KNIGHTS *and* MARTIN DEL BOSCO; *on the other,* FERNEZE)

Enter, above, BARABAS, *with a hammer, very busy; and* CARPENTERS.

BARABAS: How stand the cords? how hang these hinges? fast?
  Are all the cranes and pulleys sure?
FIRST CARPENTER: All fast.
BARABAS: Leave nothing loose, all levell'd to my mind.
  Why, now I see that you have art, indeed:
  There, carpenters, divide that gold amongst you;
(*Giving money*)
  Go, swill in bowls of sack and muscadine;
  Down to the cellar, taste of all my wines.
FIRST CARPENTER: We shall, my lord, and thank you.
(*Exeunt* CARPENTERS)
BARABAS: And, if you like them, drink your fill and die;
  For, so I live, perish may all the world!
  Now, Selim Calymath, return me word
  That thou wilt come, and I am satisfied.
Enter MESSENGER.
  Now, sirrah; what, will he come?
MESSENGER: He will; and has commanded all his men
  To come ashore, and march through Malta-streets,
  That thou mayst feast them in thy citadel.
BARABAS: Then now are all things as my wish would have 'em;
  There wanteth nothing but the governor's pelf;
  And see, he brings it.
Enter FERNEZE.
  Now, governor, the sum?
FERNEZE: With free consent, a hundred thousand pounds.
BARABAS: Pounds say'st thou, governor? well, since it is no more,
  I'll satisfy myself with that; nay, keep it still,
  For, if I keep not promise, trust not me:
  And, governor, now partake my policy.
  First, for his army, they are sent before,
  Enter'd the monastery, and underneath
  In several places are field-pieces pitch'd,
  Bombards, whole barrels full of gunpowder,
  That on the sudden shall dissever it,
  And batter all the stones about their ears,
  Whence none can possibly escape alive:
  Now, as for Calymath and his consorts,
  Here have I made a dainty gallery,

The floor whereof, this cable being cut,
Doth fall asunder, so that it doth sink
Into a deep pit past recovery.
Here, hold that knife; and, when thou seest he comes,

(*Throws down a knife*)

And with his bassoes shall be blithely set,
A warning-piece shall be shot off from the tower,
To give thee knowledge when to cut the cord,
And fire the house. Say, will not this be brave?

FERNEZE: O, excellent! here, hold thee, Barabas;
I trust thy word; take what I promis'd thee.

BARABAS: No, governor; I'll satisfy thee first;
Thou shalt not live in doubt of any thing.
Stand close, for here they come.

(FERNEZE *retires*)

Why, is not this
A kingly kind of trade, to purchase towns
By treachery, and sell 'em by deceit?
Now tell me, worldlings, underneath the sun
If greater falsehood ever has been done?

Enter CALYMATH *and* BASSOES.

CALYMATH: Come, my companion-bassoes: see, I pray,
How busy Barabas is there above
To entertain us in his gallery:
Let us salute him.—Save thee, Barabas!

BARABAS: Welcome, great Calymath!

FERNEZE: How the slave jeers at him!

(*Aside*)

BARABAS: Will't please thee, mighty Selim Calymath,
To ascend our homely stairs?

CALYMATH: Ay, Barabas.—
Come, bassoes, ascend.

FERNEZE: (*coming forward*) Stay, Calymath;
For I will shew thee greater courtesy
Than Barabas would have afforded thee.

KNIGHT: (*within*) Sound a charge there!

(*A charge sounded within:* FERNEZE *cuts the cord; the floor of the gallery
gives way, and* BARABAS *falls into a caldron placed in a pit.
Enter* KNIGHTS *and* MARTIN DEL BOSCO.

CHRISTOPHER MARLOWE

CALYMATH: How now! what means this?

BARABAS: Help, help me, Christians, help!

FERNEZE: See, Calymath! this was devis'd for thee.

CALYMATH: Treason, treason! bassoes, fly!

FERNEZE: No, Selim, do not fly:
    See his end first, and fly then if thou canst.

BARABAS: O, help me, Selim! help me, Christians!
    Governor, why stand you all so pitiless?

FERNEZE: Should I in pity of thy plaints or thee,
    Accursed Barabas, base Jew, relent?
    No, thus I'll see thy treachery repaid,
    But wish thou hadst behav'd thee otherwise.

BARABAS: You will not help me, then?

FERNEZE: No, villain, no.

BARABAS: And, villains, know you cannot help me now.—
    Then, Barabas, breathe forth thy latest fate,
    And in the fury of thy torments strive
    To end thy life with resolution.—
    Know, governor, 'twas I that slew thy son,—
    I fram'd the challenge that did make them meet:
    Know, Calymath, I aim'd thy overthrow:
    And, had I but escap'd this stratagem,
    I would have brought confusion on you all,
    Damn'd Christian dogs, and Turkish infidels!
    But now begins the extremity of heat
    To pinch me with intolerable pangs:
    Die, life! fly, soul! tongue, curse thy fill, and die!

(*Dies*)

CALYMATH: Tell me, you Christians, what doth this
    portend?

FERNEZE: This train he laid to have entrapp'd thy life;
    Now, Selim, note the unhallow'd deeds of Jews;
    Thus he determin'd to have handled thee,
    But I have rather chose to save thy life.

CALYMATH: Was this the banquet he prepar'd for us?
    Let's hence, lest further mischief be pretended.

FERNEZE: Nay, Selim, stay; for, since we have thee here,
    We will not let thee part so suddenly:
    Besides, if we should let thee go, all's one,

For with thy galleys couldst thou not get hence,
Without fresh men to rig and furnish them.

CALYMATH: Tush, governor, take thou no care for that;
My men are all aboard,
And do attend my coming there by this.

FERNEZE: Why, heard'st thou not the trumpet sound a charge?

CALYMATH: Yes, what of that?

FERNEZE: Why, then the house was fir'd,
Blown up, and all thy soldiers massacred.

CALYMATH: O, monstrous treason!

FERNEZE: A Jew's courtesy;
For he that did by treason work our fall,
By treason hath deliver'd thee to us:
Know, therefore, till thy father hath made good
The ruins done to Malta and to us,
Thou canst not part; for Malta shall be freed,
Or Selim ne'er return to Ottoman.

CALYMATH: Nay, rather, Christians, let me go to Turkey,
In person there to mediate your peace:
To keep me here will naught advantage you.

FERNEZE: Content thee, Calymath, here thou must stay,
And live in Malta prisoner; for come all the world
To rescue thee, so will we guard us now,
As sooner shall they drink the ocean dry,
Than conquer Malta, or endanger us.
So, march away; and let due praise be given
Neither to Fate nor Fortune, but to Heaven.

(*Exeunt*)

A Note About the Author

Christopher Marlowe (1564–1593) was a 16th century playwright, poet, and translator. Considered to be the most famous playwright in the Elizabethan era, Marlowe is believed to have inspired major artists such as Shakespeare. Marlowe was known for his dramatic works that often depicted extreme displays of violence, catering to his audience's desires. Surrounded by mystery and speculation, Marlowe's own life was as dramatic and exciting as his plays. Historians are still puzzled by the man, conflicted by rumors that he was a spy, questions about his sexuality, and suspicions regarding his death.

A Note from the Publisher

Spanning many genres, from non-fiction essays to literature classics to children's books and lyric poetry, Mint Edition books showcase the master works of our time in a modern new package. The text is freshly typeset, is clean and easy to read, and features a new note about the author in each volume. Many books also include exclusive new introductory material. Every book boasts a striking new cover, which makes it as appropriate for collecting as it is for gift giving. Mint Edition books are only printed when a reader orders them, so natural resources are not wasted. We're proud that our books are never manufactured in excess and exist only in the exact quantity they need to be read and enjoyed.

bookfinity™

Discover more of your favorite classics with Bookfinity™.

- Track your reading with custom book lists.
- Get great book recommendations for your personalized Reader Type.
- Add reviews for your favorite books.
- AND MUCH MORE!

Visit **bookfinity.com** and take the fun Reader Type quiz to get started.

Enjoy our classic and modern companion pairings!

Classic & Modern

www.ingramcontent.com/pod-product-compliance
Lightning Source LLC
Chambersburg PA
CBHW050954050426
42337CB00051B/1142